Be a BEAST!!

E. Mll

HOW TO BECOME A

FINANCIAL
BEAST™

By

Eric S. Miller

Written By Eric S. Miller

ISBN: 978-1-937205-28-7
Published by The Econologics Institute, Florida, USA

For more information contact:

Econologics Institute
2401 West Bay Drive, Suite 603
Largo, FL 33770
727-588-1540
info@econologics.com
www.FinancialBeastBook.com

Eric S. Miller is a Registered Financial Consultant® (RFC) and holds a Series 65 license. He is also a licensed insurance agent for life, health and variable annuity insurance. Eric is a co-owner, Managing Member and Chief Financial Advisor at Econologics Financial Advisors, LLC ('EFA'), which is registered with the Securities and Exchange Commission as an investment advisor. (Such registration does not imply a certain level of skill or training.) This communication is not an offer to sell or effect any transaction in securities or to give individualized investment advice. Neither EFA nor its affiliates provide legal, tax or accounting advice. Please consult a qualified attorney or accountant.

Table of Contents

Preface

3 Key Lessons I've Learned Working with Healthcare Practice Owners for Over a Decade

Some research indicates most children know what their purpose is in life by the time they are 4 years old. I guess I was a late bloomer because I didn't know my purpose until I was 32. At that time, I had a natural curiosity about money and finances, but it never really manifested into much financial success. I struggled financially like everyone else. Most of what I learned about money came from simple observation, self-study and mistakes. It wasn't until 2008 and the first great recession in my lifetime when I became more aware that I could have a positive impact on the financial decisions and actions of others. That moment was a catalyst in my life and I took responsibility to learn more about personal finances and to get better at helping others have more competence, confidence and control of their money.

So in 2008, I joined a financial firm with some of my colleagues. We determined our focus would be to advise practice owners in various healthcare industries on how to improve the financial condition of their household. I studied all the Certified Financial Planner® courses to learn the basics of finances and the standard methods of providing comprehensive financial advice. I set out to apply what I learned to these practice owners in financial areas such as saving for retirement, investing and insurance, to name a few. As I learned more about the financial obstacles practice owners faced, I discovered the financial progress of most of these practitioners was tied directly to the viability of their business. I quickly realized they couldn't be advised like "everyone else." Unfortunately, the CFP® curriculum provided me with no direction on how to help a veterinarian, physical therapist, dentist, chiropractor, optometrist or other medical professional deal with real world and real time financial issues, nor did it give me any data on how to properly utilize their biggest investment — their practice.

Here was the first lesson I learned:

To really make an impact on the financial lives of my clients (healthcare business owners), I had to know something about how the main wealth building engine of their household, the business, actually worked.

So I immersed myself in understanding how a private practice operated. I listened, observed, asked questions, and found out what areas of a healthcare business created its value. Surprisingly, the primary value drivers I uncovered were consistent among the various professions. Some had higher or lower overhead costs in different areas, but the successful basics needed were still the same: An effective management system, coordinated personnel, purpose driven leadership, high production targets, continuous marketing and promotion, excellent service, aggressive collections, controlled finances and reinvestment in staff training. I've since learned that when these areas are fully developed, they will always lead to a more profitable, sustainable and valuable business.

As I learned more about what areas made a practice more valuable, I was better able to communicate with my clients and convince them to harness the practice profits to better serve the financial goals of the household. It wasn't easy. It took a lot of hand-holding and accountability calls to get clients to take the necessary actions that would make a meaningful difference in their lives.

It was at this time when I learned my second lesson:

Most practice owners are not living up to their full financial potential because they are following a system that wasn't built for their success.

We live in a world where less than half of 1% of people have enough in income, assets and resources to withstand the effects of one lawsuit, one major health issue, one stock market crash or one full government shutdown.

Our economy is controlled by multiple institutions. Seemingly separate, they are all on a mission to extract as much wealth as possible so they can control the individual. This is accomplished through different economic systems. A tax system that penalizes the productive and gives to the unproductive; both rich and poor. A monetary system which slowly and gradually erodes the value of money. A legal system that makes it easy to sue anyone without merit. And then of course a healthcare system that invariably ends up targeting the caregivers who are earnestly trying to make people feel better and function well.

Only our full recognition of these financial enemies will allow us the fortitude and courage to do what we need to do to protect our families, communities, businesses and nation. Healthcare practice owners need a system built specifically for their success!

So how do we change our financial trajectory? That question lead to the third lesson I learned in having over 20,000 conversations with practice owner households:

The fundamental financial problem facing most practice owners is the gross underestimation of how much wealth they actually need to live the life they want to live.

My experience is that most business owners don't have a good grasp of their financial numbers — business and personal. I found that the majority of owners look at relatively insignificant numbers such as net worth, retirement account returns and credit scores. What's worse, the bulk of people who I encountered that did have a pulse on their income and expenses, *drastically underestimated* how much in assets and income they would need to build for the future. Unfortunately, the financial media has done a good job of convincing people that all they need to save is $2-3 million in retirement programs to survive without a job at age 59 $1/2$.

Practice Owners need to stop listening to the "Traditional" Financial Advice model.

These lessons were the inspiration for the principles and characteristics of becoming a Financial Beast™. We need to "up-the-game" for financial success. We need to "up-the-demand" to create more wealth. I feel it's my job to ensure healthcare practice owners know there is another level to be achieved and to provide a full list of the characteristics it takes to become a Financial Beast. It's not just about making money — it's about creating more opportunity for you, your family, your community and beyond.

I'll warn you now, becoming a Financial Beast is NOT an easy endeavor. It takes courage, persistence, intelligence and discipline. But the payoff is creating a life where you control the money game instead of it controlling you. Let's decide now to do whatever it takes to become a Financial Beast. I'll be your guide throughout this book.

You'll notice 3 main money themes throughout this book:

Something can ALWAYS be done to improve your financial condition.

Your financial condition can be fixed, it can be bettered, and it doesn't need to be stuck. You are the PRIME MOTIVATOR of change.

Any action that helps bring more financial order will help improve your outcome.

The mountain of financial "I Don't Knows" (IDK) most practice owners experience prevents them from taking an honest look at their financial condition. A Financial IDK = a Financial Confusion.

Example:

I don't know my business monthly make/break number.

I don't know my debt-free date.

I don't know if my net worth is increasing or decreasing.

I don't know how much I am paying in taxes.

I don't know how I will transition out of my business for full value.

Too many of these confusions lead to a situation where you no longer want to confront anything related to money. Inaction eventually leads to financial ruin. Therefore, anything you do which helps eliminate these financial IDKs will help bring more order and a betterment of your personal financial condition.

Every practice owner needs a BFFF (Best Financial Friend Forever).

Many of you have heard me use this term in the past. But what exactly is a BFFF? Well to me a Best Financial Friend would be someone who:

Provides correct financial guidance for your situation—not everyone else's

Doesn't allow you get distracted

Holds you accountable for your financial actions

Makes you feel confidence, not confusion

Pushes you to pull the trigger

There is a real financial crisis going on amongst practice owners. Time and indecision are not allies. Keep in mind that you are not a robot and in order for anyone to help you, they need your cooperation and participation to help reach your potential. Truthfully, you need to be a financial friend to yourself.

I am very happy you chose to read this book and I am very excited to help you make decisions and take actions towards becoming a Financial Beast!

This book is dedicated to:

I extend my thanks, appreciation and respect to all the clients, co-workers and partners I have worked with over the last couple of decades, even those I have lost contact with. You all played an important part in some way of this book being written. I'd like to especially thank the women in my life. I am surrounded by strong, competent, opinionated, stubborn and beautiful women. To my lovely wife Carlie, my business partner Diane, my executives Annette and Mendy; thank you for making sure that I know I am not the boss. Finally, I want to thank my Mom and Dad, who I simply love very much.

Chapter 1

Becoming a Financial Beast

To become a Financial Beast it's important to define exactly what that means. I am sure you can take a few guesses what being a Financial Beast might look like, but to be thorough, allow me to give you my definition so we collectively can agree this is a title worth achieving.

When you think of the term "Beast" you may get the idea of a wild animal or a crude and horrid person. This is an old definition. The new century definition of a beast is someone who has demonstrated a high degree of skill along with determination, persistence, and the will to win. In other words, being a beast is admirable and desirable. Anyone can become a beast in any endeavor they chose. Examples are sports, business, relationships, hobbies or academia.

My definition of a Financial Beast is someone who has made a commitment to not just succeed, but conquer their personal finances. Someone who has confronted the typical excuses that hold others back. A person who has developed constructive financial habits, keeps themself clear of parasitic people, has a clear and definable result they are pursuing and doesn't deviate from their plan just because success didn't happen overnight.

Being a Financial Beast is not just about making money. It's an attitude. It's a state of mind. It indicates one's ability to be in control of their personal financial condition. Simply put:

A Financial Beast is someone who does not let the outside economy affect their own personal economy.

You will never hear a Financial Beast say, "The economy is what dictates my success" or "The recession is killing me." They handle their own recessions without the need of a bail out by the Federal Reserve. Financial Beasts are productive, ethical, unreasonable and not dependent on the approval of others to reach their financial potential.

In this book, I will focus on the precise characteristics, attributes, attitudes and action steps needed to become a Financial Beast, starting with getting into Financial Beast Mode™.

If you aren't a Financial Beast now, don't sweat it. I am not here to beat you down and give you excuses. The information in this book will help you self-evaluate and correct the reasons. In my experience, the fundamental reason most people are not in beast mode boils down to this:

The financial condition you are currently experiencing is the result of the information, advice and education you had available, the decisions you have made, and the actions you took or didn't take. Is that a fair assessment? Although worry, anxiety and fear are typically the catalyst for change, it actually takes imagination, courage, persistence and correct information on personal economics. Changing your trajectory will take knowing exactly what the optimum result should look like and the correct estimation of effort to get there.

As a Financial Beast, here is a description of what your financial life should look like:

- You are confident in your decisions and are relaxed about money.
- You have a business or a practice which is profitable, sustainable and valuable.
- You are creating multiple and reliable income streams outside of your business.
- You are free of destructive debt.
- You have a coordinated and competent team of advisors.

- You are operating on a plan with measurable results.

- Your assets are reasonably protected from taxes, inflation and lawsuits

- You have created time to pursue other enjoyment in life and are helping others do the same.

This could be considered the full definition of financial freedom. Contrary to popular finance doctrine, realizing this status doesn't need to take 30 years to achieve. Those of you courageous enough to own a "viable business" (one that generates over $1,000,000 in revenue with more than 2 employees) can do this in 7-10 years. This level of financial success will require an understanding of how much in income, assets and resources you need to attain Financial Beast status. The amount of wealth required will vary from person to person, the characteristics will not.

Just imagine what your life would look like if all of these goals were achieved. Read them again. Close your eyes and imagine how free you would feel. Imagine how many pleasurable moments you could experience with your family, and imagine how many people you could help if you had time to pursue what is most important to you.

Word to the wise: your financial expansion does not come overnight, it doesn't always feel like you are winning and it doesn't come without battle scars. Expect opposition, expect criticism and be prepared to cut ties with people you thought were friends and allies. Regardless what the majority of people will say to the contrary (and they will), becoming a Financial Beast is a virtuous, divine and righteous pursuit.

Start it now.

Chapter 2

Handling the External Barriers

Saying there are barriers to financial success is not a profound statement. Anyone who has started a business knows the mountain of resistance and problems which crop up when you are attempting to do something which will expand your net worth and financial status. It's just part of the game. But like any game, if you are going to win, you need to KNOW your opponent, the barriers they pose and how to play the game. If you are going to win the financial game you first must identify your opponents and then strategize how you can navigate the barriers they pose. Some of these opponents are external and some are hidden; both have an agenda to relieve you of your wealth.

This chapter will address the external factors while the next chapter will deal with the hidden internal barriers keeping you from becoming a Financial Beast.

The Default Plan

We live in a society run by systems. That wouldn't be a problem if these systems were built for the people to be free and prosperous. These systems may have been set up for benevolent reasons, but over time have been usurped by those with a misunderstanding of what wealth is and where is comes from. Wealth is not money. If it were, we would never need to go to work and the government could just print our way to prosperity. Wealth is the ability to create valuable goods and services that can be exchanged for money. Wealth comes in many forms, but it ALWAYS creates something which is valuable, desirable or needed by others. Unfortunately, the majority of these institutional systems have built-in barriers that prevent prosperity for the people. Let's examine a few and why:

Financial System

First, it is important to realize that Central Banks are set up in every country and all coordinate with one another. Aside from North Korea and Iran, all other countries are part of this global banking system which is "supported" by the Bank of International Settlements, which offers banking services and a forum to discuss monetary and regulatory policies to these banks. These policies have a direct effect on the value of currency and the rate of economic growth. Further, the entire financial system is set up and operated on the concept of Fractional Reserve Banking. That is just a fancy way of saying that banks are allowed to lend out well in excess of the amount of actual deposits on hand.

Monetary and Lending system: We have a monetary system that one in a million people can actually understand and explain the mechanics of how it works. Unfortunately, the results are very observable. The cost of goods and services is going up, the small businesses who produce these goods and services are being squeezed and forced into closing down or consolidating into big corporations, the amount of debt people carry is at record levels, and the buying power of our currency is diminishing every year. A monetary and lending system that operates like this punishes people who save money and bails out those who are part of its inner circle.

Investment System: "Stocks only go up" is the mantra of today. According to a study I read In 2021, there was more money that flowed into the stock market in 5 months than all of the last 12 years combined. With bank interest rates at record lows, most people felt the only option is to put their money into public securities for FOMO (fear of missing out). In addition, the proliferation of online brokerage services and social media "experts" has turned investing into speculating with no regard for what a company actually produces and how well managed it may or may not be.

Why is this a barrier?

This financial system is designed to make the currencies of the world easy to control. Governments can have the banks create more money to fund whatever will keep bureaucrats in control and banks flush with interest payments. It also causes massive inequities in that it punishes people who are not first in line to receive the money. It causes a phenomena called inflation which is simply a condition where there is more money in the system compared to the goods and services. This causes prices to go up in an artificial manner and eventually ends with a debasement of the currency and social unrest.

Tax System

Our tax system is set up to provide cover for 2 classes of people: the very rich and the very poor. The tax system is designed to penalize productive people and reward those who don't produce; both rich and poor. Even though the proponents of our tax system say it was set up to "tax the rich" (as if making $400,000 actually makes you rich), it actually does the exact opposite. *Our tax system does not tax the rich, it taxes the productive*. The small business owners who make between $400,000–$1,000,000 a year in personal income are the targets. They end up paying the highest **percentage** of their income to taxes.

Why is this a barrier?

Taxes for those that make over $300,000 a year are usually about 30% of your overall income. It is a huge expense and is made intentionally difficult to navigate.

Legal System

It's easy to make lawyer jokes. But there is nothing funny about the threat of having your assets ripped from you. Our system does make it rather simple to file a lawsuit against anyone and, whether you are guilty or innocent, you have to have resources to defend yourself. The emotional and financial effects of a lawsuit can be disastrous. As people become poorer and more desperate, they look to those who "have money" as their ticket out of poverty. In a society where being a victim is celebrated, the legal system makes it simple to be subject to a lawsuit, whether warranted or not, and force you to have to bear the costs of defending yourself.

Why is this a barrier?

As people become poorer through inflation and there are less job opportunities, they can become desperate. In this desperation, they will attack those who they perceive to have resources. That could be you.

Healthcare System

Our nation is unhealthy in so many ways. Political divide and class warfare are viruses driven by hidden provocateurs who, as Alfred said to Bruce Wayne in the movie *The Dark Knight* when referencing the Joker, "Just want to see the world burn." But a nation is as wealthy as it has people who are able and willing to produce. The majority of what is pushed by our healthcare system to "treat" maladies is drugs and surgeries. Of course these are needed in some capacity, but the overall physical fitness of most Americans is staggeringly bad. This presents an enormous cost to the taxpayers to take care of all its citizens which means the amount of borrowing to serve the healthcare sector will only drive costs up.

Why is this a barrier?

For those of you in the healthcare system, you know that private practice is under fire. Big corporations make deals with big governments which seek to commoditize services and deliver them at prices that makes is difficult for private practices to compete. The increase in regulatory requirements make it equally difficult by adding additional expenses and draining resources. In the end, the system is attacking the very people who are providing the care: healthcare business owners.

These systems have a very specific plan for you. Make interest rates so low to entice you to burden yourself with massive amounts of debt. Tell you the government will bail you out with stimulus checks. Punish you for saving money. Force you to invest in areas you really don't understand just to keep up with inflation, and create a tax code which is so rooted in complexity and fear, that you will always comply and pay the maximum amount to the IRS. Ugh. This is the default financial plan.

I can validate this because every year when we bring in new clients, I see the same thing on their personal financial statements. More debt, less liquid money, brokerage and retirement accounts with massive concentration in stocks, and huge tax bills. That kind of plan won't get you into Beast Mode, it will get you into Broke Mode.

Chapter 3

Your Check-Up from the Neck-Up: Hidden Barriers

You certainly have external financial enemies, however, the biggest financial barriers facing you will be the ones created in that 7-inch space between the neck and the top of your head. Whenever I have encountered someone in a poor financial condition, 99% of the time it was NOT based upon outside factors; it was an inside job. Here are 3 hidden factors we do to ourselves that bar us from financial independence:

1. Self-Sabotage

We can all remember a time when we tried to help someone with a problem. You enlightened them on the problem, presented a solution, and gave them the exact sequence of actions which would alleviate the problem. It seemed so simple what the person needed to do. And they go and do the exact opposite. That is self-sabotage. Most of the time, the destructive actions we do to ourselves are sitting below our awareness level. This is the reason we continue the self-sabotage. Take a look at everything you feel is non-optimum about your financial situation and you may uncover some things you are doing which are contributing to the condition. You are not helpless against your own actions, and you can control your bad habits.

2. Limiting Beliefs

We have been fed "beliefs" on different topics our whole life. They may come from parents, friends, gurus, media or religious figures. Having beliefs is not necessarily a bad thing. It is those beliefs which limit your aspirations that can be particularly harmful. When you hear someone say "You only need so much money," "Expansion always brings headaches," or "You only live once so spend it now," you are dealing with limiting financial beliefs. The truth is we put a cap on how much we think we can accomplish. You will exert the exact amount of effort needed to accomplish whatever goals you have. I am not saying everyone has the capability of becoming a billionaire, but you have more in you than what most people tell you is achievable. Move the goalposts back a bit and you will find a greater degree of happiness and achievement.

3. Not taking responsibility for the financial damage we have caused others.

By and large, when I find people who are struggling with their finances, their business, and have an impulse to withdraw and give up the game, I generally find two things are occurring:

1. *The person is actively doing destructive and unethical activities which they are not proud of.*

2. *They have failed to rectify any financial damage they have caused other people or their family.*

Oh boy. I can hear the gears grinding now. Eric, what in the heck are you talking about?

Money is a simple game. If you are engaging in activities which are positive and constructive towards building your net worth, it will increase. If you are putting in lots of hours at work, bringing value to your clients, training your staff, building a good culture, marketing correctly, setting aside reserves, building other income sources, paying off your bad debt, minimizing your taxes legally, investing in actual investments which pay you to own them, you treat people well and root out toxic people from your life, you will see your personal finances flourish.

If however, you complain all the time, watch YOUTUBE videos seven hours a day, check in at 10:00am and leave at 4:00pm with a 2-hour lunch, drink or do drugs excessively, cheat on your spouse or act promiscuous, cheat on your taxes, overbill your clients, allow incompetency in your business, overburden yourself with debts, save nothing and spend everything you make on depreciating stuff,chances are you will suffer in financial ruin.

As to my second point, another method to get back on the right track is to rectify any financial damage you may have caused others. Don't overthink this. Maybe there was someone you borrowed money from and didn't pay them back. Maybe there was a time you took money that wasn't yours. Maybe you overspent on something you shouldn't have. Whatever it was, just try and make up for it. It is one thing to admit you did something wrong, but you don't truly handle a situation until you take responsibility for the negative effect you created. It can be as simple as writing a letter to someone apologizing for screwing them over or sending a check for $20 to your mom. JUST DO SOME KIND OF ACTION to show that you are attempting to make up for a wrong you committed.

It will be gratifying to build your financial empire on clean soil and a clean heart. One of my friends was not where he wanted to be in his finances or his life. He drank to excess, cheated on his taxes and his wife, and never kept his word. To his credit, he confronted things he was doing which contributed to the condition he was in. He suffered greatly for a period of time. Eight years later, he has a happy marriage, a business worth $15 million, and pride in himself. None of us our saints. **We don't have to**

be perfect, but we do have to recognize there is a correlation between our personal actions and the current state of our financial affairs.

The Game of Money does have opponents and it's best to know their playbook. If you don't have a plan to take control of your finances then the banking system, tax system, investment system and legal system will slowly bleed you dry. Be a true financial friend to yourself and evaluate those things you are doing which you are not proud of. Make sure you clean up any negative financial situation with people you have taken advantage of, caused an unfavorable result with or have ripped off. Remember, it is easy to blame the outside economy for your current problems, but it is almost always an inside job. Getting into Financial Beast Mode does require a look in the mirror. Just remember, ANYTHING can be fixed.

Chapter 4

The Fuel of Financial Beast Mode: Purpose and Decision

Don't worry, I am not about to go full Tony Robbins mode and give you an uplifting and motivating essay on the power of purpose and decisions. I will say they are **absolutely necessary** for you to be able to withstand the fury of resistance you will receive on your financial journey.

Purpose

The basic meaning of "purpose" is the reason for which something exists or is done. Its derivation (root meaning) comes from the Old French word *proposer: to propose, set forth.* I am sure you have heard the phrase "Money Motivated" many times. I dare say the most successful financial individuals are purpose driven rather than money driven. Having a purpose is what propels someone. It is the force behind the action. It also allows someone to overcome the obstacles that are present in one's journey. If you encounter someone who doesn't have a purpose, it is indeed a sad sight to see.

They are easily manipulated, prone to destructive behavior and will change directions repeatedly. Your purpose for achieving financial success will be necessary for you to establish early on. It needs to be powerful enough to push through the boring and repetitive tasks it takes to achieve the next level. Most healthcare practice owners have a purpose to help as many patients as they can to improve their health and create a business which provides financial security for their employees and their families. That is a noble purpose.

To demonstrate importance of this, when we see a practice experiencing a real cash flow crunch, the FIRST order of business is to make sure every person in the organization understands the purpose of the organization. Done correctly, you will see this actually brings the organization back to life! People will be moving faster and completing their tasks because they are reinvigorated as to why they chose to work for you.

Human beings do not function well without having a motivation. This is why the idle rich and inheritances cases can be the most psychotic, unstable, unethical and unproductive people you will ever meet. Giving your kids unlimited and unearned money, cars and luxury items without assisting them in finding their purpose in life is equally cruel. Having money just for the sake of having money is not a purpose.

Decision

When one is making a decision, they are settling something which is in dispute or doubt. It comes from the Latin word *decedere: literally, to cut off.* When you make a real decision, you are cutting off from all of those things which caused the doubt or dispute in the first place. It can be as simple as making a decision to have a tuna sandwich instead of a pizza. I am cutting off the possibility of eating pizza because I made a decision to eat healthy. Making constructive financial decisions is powerful. They allow you to minimize your distractions and focus on those things which lead to wins. Take this example I received from a Physical Therapy owner a few years ago:

> *"Wanted to share with you that I am 100% debt-free as of yesterday. I remember going to your course in 2011 as a new practice owner — I set a goal to be debt-free at 45 years old and thought to myself — that is a steep goal — I just turned 44 and have no debt and 2 homes paid for. Thanks for your help."*

He made a decision to be debt-free and took the necessary steps to achieve a debt free status. He had to make some sacrifices, but for him it was worth it.

When you make the decision to get into Financial Beast Mode, you may have to cut off old habits, old beliefs, and disconnect from people who are not going in the same direction as you. This includes accountants, advisors, and other professionals who you thought you could depend upon. Getting into a Financial Beast Mode requires an attitude of necessity that some people who are operating on the 30-year retirement model cannot handle. It's Ok to let them go.

As a final point, don't assume that every decision you make as a business owner is going to be correct. It won't be. The good news is that your financial life is not a best-out-of-a-100 where 90/100 gets you an A. Life seems to be more forgiving. You just need to be right 51% of the time to win the game. Of course, we all want to be right in our decision-making process more than 51%, but you have a little more leeway than you thought.

Know your purpose, trust yourself, be thoughtful, analyze data, but be fast in making decisions. Unlike what you have heard about the power of time and compounding interest, time is not a friend of those who want to get into Financial Beast Mode.

Chapter 5

The 7 Zones of Financial Independence

Rich vs. Poor is a powerful dichotomy. It has been used by politicians and master manipulators to create conflicts and punish countless people. The reality is there are many different levels to the money game.

Think of it this way: if you are interested in becoming an expert in karate, you first start out as white belt, then yellow, orange, green, blue, brown and finally black. Each level has its own challenges and barriers, as well as skills one must learn and apply in order to progress to the next. You can't go from a novice white belt to an expert black belt without going THROUGH the other levels. Your financial condition is no different. But to start, you MUST know which financial zone you are currently in so you can map out the steps required for the next zone.

The road to financial independence is open to those who completely recognize where they are compared to where they are headed.

Allow me to first outline a few of the characteristics of each of the different financial zones.

Personal Income

This is the amount of personal income typically made by individuals in this zone. The income can come from any source but the amounts for most people in this zone are pretty consistent.

Net Worth

The net worth of an individual is simply the value of one's assets (business value, real estate values, investment accounts) minus the liabilities (debts) one owes. It's a fairly simple calculation and, while you will hear most "gurus" clamor about net worth, let me assure you, I have met many people who had a high net worth but very low income, and vice versa. Those instances aside, one's net worth is a useful calculation to measure one's financial zone.

Consumer Debt/Income Producing Debt

There are two types of debt one can have. The first type is consumer debt, which is debt that doesn't provide income and appreciate in value. Examples are a primary residence, second home, credit cards and auto loans. The second type is income-producing debt. This is debt used to purchase an asset which will provide cash flow and increase in value. Examples are business ownership, commercial real estate, multi-family rental units, etc.

Number of Income Streams

It isn't breaking news that having multiple income streams is ideal and important. However, most people are trying to solve the problem of not having multiple income streams with impatient speculation. That being said, as one moves up the financial zones, the opportunity for multiple streams of income arises.

Financial Condition

This is the overall state of one's financial affairs. How it is operating, its appearance, quality and working order.

Number of Americans in this Range

How do you know what kind of financial condition you are in if you don't evaluate the number of people who are statistically in this zone? This is simple to measure utilizing IRS statistics.

Effective Tax Rate

This is the average rate of tax one generally can expect to pay as a percentage of their total income. It does not include state taxes, as those are too variable to include.

As a word of caution, none of these financial zones and associated numbers are absolute. There will be statistical outliers. This was developed based upon IRS statistics, financial data from 350 business owner households, deductive calculations based on income from business earnings, and my observations of individuals who are super wealthy, productive, unproductive and poor.

Let's take a look at the definition of each zone:

Zone 0: Trapped

Aside from those born into wealth, Zone 0 is where everyone starts. Unfortunately, too many people remain in this condition. In this zone, the income of the majority is in a range from $0–$50,000. If you are a business owner, most of your staff probably resides here. People in this zone typically have a negative net worth. This means they generally don't own many assets or have much in liquid assets. Almost all the debt in this zone is consumer debt. The only income stream is the wage they earn at their job or by governmental assistance. The amount of tax which people pay would generally be less than 10%. The main money attitudes of most people in this zone is "I cannot have money," "I am a failure," or "I cannot work or create money."

The financial condition in this zone is "trapped." Trapped in a job that doesn't pay the bills, trapped by creditors, trapped in a house they can't move from, and trapped in a negative mindset where they have given up on achieving any kind of financial success. The most depressing aspect of this zone is the sheer number of people that sit in this zone. Of the 350,000,000 Americans, 75% or 270,000,000 Americans are stuck in this zone. There is a way out of this zone. The first step is your recognition that you are in this zone and being stuck here is not inevitable.

Zone 1: Scarcity

When you graduate from being financially trapped, you will move up to Zone 1. Most people in this zone are making between $50,000–$200,000. While this seems like a large income range, the overall condition for most households is not strikingly different. If you are a business owner, some of your best technical employees, executives and associates will be in this range. A lot of solo entrepreneurs who have two employees or less are in this range. These are typically people who have some type of technical or college training. The net worth of people in this zone is anywhere between $0–$1,000,000. Almost all the debt that people have in this range is still consumer debt. The cars may be nicer, the houses may be bigger, but the type of debt is still the same. There is also a much higher amount of student debt.

Most people in this zone are still reliant on one income stream which comes in the form of wage earnings from their duties as an employee. The operative word that best describes the attitude of this zone is "scarcity." There is never enough and every financial decision is made with the mindset of "either/or." The either/or mindset is the indicator that proves a scarcity of money exists. As a financial advisor, it is here where I field questions such as, "Should I pay off debt OR put money in savings?," "Should I pay for college OR put money into retirement?," "Should I put money in my 401k OR build up my emergency fund?." This is symptomatic of a scarcity condition because you should be able to do BOTH. The money attitudes of most in this zone is "I have an uncertain financial future," "I depend upon others to create my wealth," and "I don't know who to trust with money." The effective tax rate is generally between 15–20%, and the number of Americans who are in this range is 35,000,000 or 20% of the population.

If you are doing the math, 95% of ALL Americans or 332,000,000 are in Zone 0 or Zone 1.

Zone 2: Insecure

As one begins to climb the financial ladder, they can expect to hit a zone which looks pretty appealing to most people. This is because Zone 2 is one that only about 14,000,000 Americans enjoy and where the personal income ranges between $200,000 and $400,000. This zone is where one could observe a lot of successful professionals, private practice owners, skilled sales people, executives and small business owners with between 5-10 employees. About 80% of the debt that people carry in this zone is still consumer debt, because as people improve their condition there is a tendency to acquire a better "quality" of this bad debt. However, 20% of the debt for those in this zone is income producing (good) debt, which includes purchasing smaller rental units, smaller commercial buildings or business acquisition loans (buying existing small businesses). The net worth of people in this zone ranges between one million and three million, typically from savings and retirement investments, home ownership, business ownership, and real estate ownership.

It is in this zone where you see an individual begin to slowly create additional income streams or have the desire to create multiple cash flows. Even though the financial condition is much better in Zone 2, the condition is still considered to be "insecure." Therefore, there is still a large dependency on the main money artery, which is typically their primary business. The money attitude of the majority of people in this zone is still scarcity because people will tend to spend exactly what they make and then some.

Zone 3: Content

Here we have the zone that is considered the most dangerous of them all: Zone 3. This may seem a bit contradictory because the income level for most people in this zone is between $400,000 and $1,000,000. This IS the 1%; known as the most vilified group in America because they seem to "have it all," but only do so on the backs of the little guy. Of course this is not true; they work hard for their wealth! The people in this zone tend to pay the highest percent of their income to taxes. One of the more unfortunate qualities of this group is they tend to rely on the advice of the traditional financial advisor or accountant. This puts the people in this zone in jeopardy because that common advice instructs them to "buy a big home, put money into your 401k, buy stocks, buy term insurance and invest the difference and don't mess with the IRS." The people in this zone are very susceptible to the opinions of those who reside in a lower zone, and it is those "lower zone" people who cannot relate to challenges or opportunities people in this Zone 3 face.

The word that best describes the condition of people in this zone is "contentment." Because of the extreme hard work it took to get to into this zone, most people stop pushing at this point. The attitude is "I have just enough money" and because most of their friends are in the zone below them, people in Zone 3 tend to start to relax and enjoy the good life. They buy bigger homes, second homes and more "stuff." Their debt ratio is usually 50% consumer debt and 50% income producing debt. This is the zone that most traditional financial advisors try to get their clients into and proclaim they are "financially secure." This is false. With a net worth of between three million and six million, the people in this zone cannot afford to make a mistake with their investments, their practice or their health. One bad move and they are right down into a lower zone again.

Zone 4 and 5: Expansion and Abundance.

Zones 4 and 5 are where true financial freedom begins. This is where one can really start to see individuals creating an abundance of income. While in Zone 4, the main money artery, the primary business, still provides the majority of the income; however, you do start to see significant income streams being built in other businesses, investment accounts, insurance products, alternatives and real estate. The business owner in this zone is generally not working as a technician of any kind and is acting primarily as a CEO to guide the expansion of the business. The business earnings are significant enough that the value is a multiple of anywhere between 6–12 times EBITDA (earnings before interest, tax, depreciation and amortization).

As the business owner expands their empire, the income and net worth accelerate at a rapid pace. The quality of their "opportunities" are the best of the best. This is because the person in zone 4 or 5 has situated themselves in a position where they attract more viable possibilities to grow. People in these zones are considered "lucky" or have "all the right connections." The truth is, they are presented with an abundance of fruitful opportunities because they are being rewarded for helping so many people (through their services and employment of the community). The general money attitude for most in these zones is "I will always have money" and with a net worth of over twenty million, they can afford to take a calculated risk or make a financial mistake and not fall into a lower condition. It is in these 2 zones where you see one's net worth continue to rise exponentially. In fact, there are so many income streams for people in these zones that they will never need to be concerned about financial insecurity.

Zone 6 and 7: Power and Indestructible Wealth

There are probably less than 10,000 people in America who will ever get to enjoy these 2 zones. Within these zones you will find two types of people. The first type consists of individuals who create a huge value to their customers through their legitimate business activity. The second type is a faction who tries to collect as much wealth as possible at your expense. They believe in the zero sum gain, which means in order for them to win you have to lose. The majority of the people in this zone are the first type, own the majority shares of their companies and have created multiple income streams in other ventures. They have attracted enough attention where their products and brands are extremely well known and utilized, and they have acquired this status fairly. **This truly is financial power!**

In this zone, people have so much wealth that nothing could endanger their financial survival regardless of what happens to the economy at large. **Their wealth is indestructible**. A telling statistic is the amount of tax individuals pay relative to their income in these zones. Typically, they will hire some kind of "family office" with a team of financial experts on their payroll. In these rare cases they are able to set up multiple entities to defer or minimize their tax liabilities through the use of advanced tax strategies. Charitable foundations, 1031 exchanges, Captive Insurance Companies, and many other strategies are used by these people in these zones with no fear of being audited or harassed by the IRS.

They understand the value of money. Their money attitude is "I am a creator of wealth" and "I am creating amazing effects with my wealth." People in this zone are typically philanthropic. It is commonplace for them to donate an enormous sum of money to charities. They know their potential and will disagree with the status quo. They have taken ungodly risks and are not afraid to go to the financial brink. The most admirable quality of these people is their attitude that they have acquired enormous wealth and want others to have wealth, too. For those who have achieved this zone under no unfair practices, one can observe them to be the ones who truly represent the best of mankind.

What's next? First, you must be very clear on what financial zone you are in and truly begin to understand your current financial condition, and then look at the next higher financial zone. Determine what it will take to reach that next level and work with a guide who can help you map out a plan on how to achieve it. Getting into a financial condition of truly unlimited wealth does take time. It is based on *taking small repetitive and boring steps in the beginning to put you in a position to pounce on real opportunities to accelerate your wealth building.* You determine how long it takes to get there by your persistence, imagination and activity.

Download the chart I created that illustrates these financial zones, print it off and post it in your office. The visual reminder can serve as a great motivator to keep you on track to become a Financial Beast.

To download the 7 Zones of Financial Freedom whitepaper, or to schedule a free 30-minute consultation, use this link or scan the QR code below: www.FinancialBeastBook.com

Chapter 6

Welcome to the Resistance

Ask anyone who has engaged in an activity for any length of time and they will tell you that patterns become noticeable to them. These are observable phenomena which become transparent to someone because of the amount of time and attention they have focused on an activity. Whether it's a computer programmer, a pro-athlete, an executive, a police officer or a business consultant, they can recall certain patterns they've observed while honing their craft. Make no mistake, they don't create the patterns, they simply observe whatever truth is present.

As a financial advisor, there is no pattern I have noticed more prominently than the TSUNAMI of RESISTANCE that happens to a business owner when they start implementing strategies that will shake the status quo of the business and household. This disruption of change in financial operations that will set the owner on to the next level is not met with rainbows and unicorns. Instead, it is met with major resistance in the form of disasters, pushback and criticism at every turn. It has been the most startling phenomena I have seen because it happens EVERY TIME. To every client. No exceptions.

This resistance pattern can be observed at the onset of any financial or business activity that would bring more order, expansion, value and wealth to someone. This resistance doesn't seem to play favorites and it doesn't matter what financial zone you're in. When you begin to implement financial activities that are expansive in nature, you will be met with a wave of very unpleasant and resistive factors that will make it appear as though you made the wrong decision.

Let me give you an example. The first financial action I have every practice owner client implement is expensing their practice profits to the household. This is done by setting up a "Wealth Storage Account" where we start a scheduled distribution of up to 10% of gross collections. The purpose of these funds is to be invested outside of the business to create additional income streams.

Even though this is a very disruptive financial activity and puts a lot of pressure on the business cash flow, the mechanics of it are stupid simple. It's as easy as opening an outside bank account and setting up a systematic weekly expense payment to that account in QuickBooks. What could possibly go wrong? EVERYTHING!

In my 13+ years of working with healthcare business owners, I have done this hundreds of times. I cannot recall one time where the implementation of this one simple (yet disruptive) action wasn't met with some sort of obstacle or problem that caused the owner to pause and wonder if he or she was doing the wrong thing. Here is just a sample of the resistance I've seen happen when we start putting in financial order:

- ✓ The power went out at the practice owner's office when the application was being taken (this has happened over 10 times since to other owners).

- ✓ An office manager or key employee quits.

- ✓ An unexpected bill shows up for thousands of dollars.

- ✓ A key piece of equipment breaks down unexpectedly.

- ✓ The practice owner's car breaks down or gets a flat tire.

- ✓ The bank check sent to open the wealth storage account gets lost in the mail.

- ✓ Termite damage is discovered at the practice owner's home costing thousands in repairs.

- ✓ A key appliance breaks or the roof leaks.

- ✓ The owner experiences the worst cash flow month ever.

✓ The hot water heater breaks or the basement floods.

✓ The accountant tells the owner it will increase their taxes and hurt the business.

I could go on and on. Here's the point: your decisions are very powerful! When you make a decision to take your business and personal finances to the next level, you are going against the status quo of comfort. For some reason, when a person makes a decision to expand, they are met with a wave of resistance. This resistance wave comes in many forms and is designed to make you question your decision. It may even hit you so hard that you want to give up. I don't know WHY this occurs. I just know that it does — every time. This is not a religious or metaphysical discussion of the origins of life or the impact of a higher power, it's a pattern I've observed to be true.

It's my opinion that when we decide to conquer a task or create a new habit, it must be met with some amount of resistance to prove we are on the right path. It validates the forward motion will be meaningful and have an impact for the greater good. When was the last time you did something that created a HUGE effect in your life? Was it easy? I doubt it. But if the impact was huge, then the resistance you overcame made it worthwhile. I'm here to tell you to push through the resistance.

Expect it. It's actually a good sign. The good news is it doesn't last very long. Be persistent and you will start to see the results of your disruptive (expansive) activities right away!

A Financial Beast welcomes resistance because the result of pushing through is so powerful! You may be asking yourself what are the disruptive financial or business activities which bring on this resistance wave. Although not all actions have the same level of importance, I've listed some I have witnessed create a tsunami of resistance.

Disruptive Financial and Business Activities that Create a Resistance Wave:

- Implementing an effective practice management system.

- Starting multiple locations.

- Buying a commercial building.

- Remodeling the facility.

- Rechanneling business cash flow to the household at the correct magnitude (10% of business revenue).

- Putting in good financial policy in the household and the business.

- Setting correct targets for increased income for the business and household.

- Deciding to hit a net worth goal that is higher than you ever dreamed possible.

- Hiring an associate doctor.

- Hiring executives for the business.

- Joining a mastermind group for expansion and growth accountability.

- Following an accelerated debt payoff schedule.

- Selling your business.

- Changing a member of owner's financial team such as an accountant, financial advisor, attorney, etc.

- Reallocating retirement account assets.

- Increasing the marketing budget to 10% of practice revenue.

- And so many more...

How do you survive the resistance wave? The funny thing about the resistance wave is that it really can't hurt you. I promise it will not cause your eyes to bleed or put you into a zombie-like state. It will test your resolve. It will test relationships of people you thought cared about you (family included) and it will make you feel like you are suffocating and trapped. This is just an illusion. There is no situation you cannot get out of. It is heartbreaking to watch someone give up or, worse yet, not even try because they listened to the "feedback" of someone who has already given up on their dreams.

Put your nose to the grindstone, keep doing the actions which are in front of you, COMPLETE those actions and don't quit. When the resistance passes, you will be the beneficiary of the increased amount of financial freedom. Rest assured, every financial level has obstacles, criticisms and resistance. The financial rewards are worth the effort. However, the pride, self-confidence, self-awareness and ability you procure will far outweigh any monetary gains. Push through the resistance wave and you will become the Financial Beast you never imagined possible!

Chapter 7

The Magic Money Triangle: Be an ACE with Money

There are plenty of advertisements for books, seminars and conferences promoting how to "beat the system" and "build wealth." I have yet to see the majority succeed with these fly-by-night programs. If you want to get into Financial Beast Mode, you must first recognize that learning these principles is both science and art. The science is based on basic fundamentals which you cannot ignore. The art is how skillfully you utilize these fundamental principles and accelerate your ability to increase your income, assets and resources. Anyone can learn the fundamental principles of a sport or game, but those who practice become the most competent and the ones who generally end up winning.

The fundamentals of money can be learned and are actually based on a simple triangle called ACE.

Imagine each point of the triangle represents a certain skill which you must become good at if you want to have financial independence. The A stands for Acquisition of Money. The C represents Control of Money, and the E is for Expansion of Money. If you examine most truly wealthy people, you will discover each found a way to master all three of these skills.

A = Acquisition of Money

There is more money in circulation now than there has ever been in human history. You don't have to "make money," you must learn how to *acquire* it. Hundreds of BILLIONS of dollars are spent in the fields of physical therapy, optometry, veterinary, chiropractic, podiatry, and dentistry every single year. Therefore, if you own a practice in these or similar industries, you have a golden opportunity to acquire some of this circulating money. The first aspect of acquiring money is having the correct target of how much your business needs to produce to fulfill your financial goals. Most people drastically underestimate their targets.

In addition to operating your business on the right targets, you might want to look into areas where you are missing opportunity. For a business owner, **there is no greater expense than income that should have been made, but wasn't.** Most businesses don't spend enough on marketing to expand their reach to their audience. In addition, be sure ALL of your staff have skills to sell and overcome objections so people will happily pay you. You might ask yourself, "What is the customer experience like in my business?" If you make your client/patient feel like a VIP, you will most likely have them as a constant source of revenue for life. Keep in mind though, you must be worthy of trust and create predictability in your service to the public. You may attract attention for the first transaction, but if the public loses confidence in you or your service, you could lose more than just their business.

Disney does a wonderful job of acquiring money. They promise a "magical" experience for the whole family and have no problem charging absurd amounts of money. The shiny bright smiles of young kids and the effect that has on their parents is exactly why they are a multi billion dollar company.

C = Control of Money

Money likes order. Like water flows over a collapsed dam, money will go everywhere if it is not properly channeled. Believe it or not, there are many successful healthcare practice owners who are good at getting new patients in the door and driving in revenue but are lousy at controlling money. The mechanics of controlling money are actually pretty easy to understand. Set up a method to expense EVERY dollar that comes into the organization so 98% of all of income is spent. The key is to make sure you include your profits, reserves, debt payments and tax liabilities as part of your expense method.

Another area I have found where money gets "lost" is allowing irresponsible individuals to have access to your money lines. You should have tight reigns over anyone who manages your money or is responsible for the collection of your revenue. When hiring a CFO, collections or financial management person, you want an absolute bulldog personality controlling your finances. Someone who doesn't accept excuses as to why there is no money flowing into your organization. Most successful practice owners closely monitor their financial statements at minimum once a week. The control of money is mostly a mindset of your right to keep money. I'm giving you permission now to be relentless with anyone who thinks otherwise. Having wealth is your divine right. Anything that indicates otherwise is a violation of your integrity as a professional.

E = Expansion of Money

Holding on to too much cash is not a good strategy for money expansion. At the same time, to make a big play, you do need reserves or access to capital. Far too many practice owners do not prudently invest their money. They tend to over-speculate in areas where they don't have control of the outcome. I've seen the most intelligent owners chasing investment returns like they are chasing butterflies with no real understanding of the investment risk. The "trick" to expanding money is making the practice an income machine and reinvesting a portion of the profits to those activities where you have more control of the outcome. The first rule of expansion *is to not lose the money*. Preserve your reserves so you can invest to expand.

The other rule of money expansion is to invest in opportunities that compensate you to own them. Cars, boats, and lake homes don't necessarily pay you to own them; these are expenses. Your practice, commercial or rental real estate, dividend paying company stock, bonds, and other proven cash flow businesses will compensate you to own them; these are investments. The expansion of money takes a lot of courage, planning and discipline. You must be willing to say no. You also must be willing to take calculated risks. The better you get at this fundamental principle, the faster you expand your wealth.

This ACE Money Triangle is an excellent self-assessment tool that you can use whether your finances are on the rise or decline. Study it well to know what areas are strong and what needs work. Getting into Financial Beast Mode will happen much faster when you have all three operating at full power. Knowing how to acquire, control, and expand money are the building blocks of wealth building.

Chapter 8

The Parent Company

Most financially successful people would list taking care of their family as a primary motivation that drove them towards achievement. In my 20,000+ conversations with practice owners, most unequivocally said that providing a stable and safe financial environment for their family was a priority. Unfortunately, they spend all of their time in the practice, serving the needs of the business, and so treat the practice as the primary entity from which all decisions are made. This is inverse of what should be occurring. The business should serve you, not the other way around. Your "household" owns the business. Therefore, it is the household where financial decisions should be prioritized.

If you are going to become a Financial Beast, you must understand two basic truths about your Household:

1. **The household should operate like a business.**

2. **You must treat your household like a Parent Company.**

Let's further examine why this is true and why it matters to your financial success.

Your Household is the Parent Company to all other assets you own, including your practice. In corporate America there is a term called the "Parent Company." The parent company is the organization that owns or controls junior or subsidiary companies. Most businesses have a parent company they report to and where profits flow to serve the needs of that primary entity. Your household is a no different. It is in fact treated as a business in the eyes of the IRS. They assign you a tax id number (your social security number) and ask you to report all sources of income (just look at your tax return). Your household and its members control all assets owned, regardless of if you have a business, real estate, retirement accounts, bank accounts or even gold. Because of this, all valuable assets should be structured to benefit the goals and purposes of the Household and its members.

As this concept is new, most practice owners do not view their household as the parent company, nor do they run their household like a business. Therefore, the relationship between the household and the practice is that the household is subservient to the practice. When the practice is the priority, the household gets neglected in many ways. This inverse relationship causes owners to make incorrect financial decisions or omit actions which otherwise would improve their personal financial condition. This includes (but not limited to):

- Not setting up a system that flows business profits automatically to the household.

- Not building significant income sources outside of the practice.

- Overleveraging the household with too much bad debt.

- Never getting out of the practitioner role to make the business more valuable.

- Following financial advice from people who don't understand their practice.

- Not utilizing any household financial metrics to measure the financial goals of the household.

- Keeping too much cash in the business.

- Has insufficient household reserves.

- Has no impactful tax minimization strategies

- Owns valuable assets in their own name exposing them to potential loss.

- Participates in speculative investments without evaluating risk or investment policy.

- Has a partial or non-existent exit strategy to sell their business at maximum value.

- Has the majority of their retirement savings in Qualified Plans (401k's, IRA's)

- Relies mostly or solely on the financial advice from their CPA and does not have a coordinated financial team.

- Has not updated their estate plan in 5 years if at all.

- Has not determined how much in income, assets and resources they need to fund their desired lifestyle.

- Cannot easily locate important financial documents or access important investment accounts.

- Does not get regular financial guidance, follow any kind of comprehensive plan or further their financial training.

Who is Your Household Chief Financial Officer®?
Every financially successful business has an excellent Chief Financial Officer (CFO). Therefore, it stands to reason that every household needs to have ONE person in charge of making sure the household is moving in the right direction. The Household CFO® is not the person just designated to "pay the bills." They are the head honcho in charge of ensuring the Household is profitable, sustainable, solvent, protected, and transferable, and the members of the household have time free to pursue their purposes and live their desired lifestyle. They are trained, educated, and responsible for making sure the household is on track and the above points are in. They are vital to the survival of the organization they serve. This doesn't have to be a complicated position, nor

should the person try and do everything themselves. A good Household CFO has hired excellent advisors who understand their specific industry and will include financial advisors who strategize and invest, tax strategists, CPAs, bookkeepers, attorneys and other qualified competent professionals to help the household implement a comprehensive strategy.

If you want to have enough wealth to leave as a legacy, you need to make sure you are building your household empire in that direction. Stop following rank-and-file financial advice and create your own "family office" of competent advisors who want to help you on your journey. It takes a bit of work up front, but the results you can achieve will allow you to have the most important commodity you could hope for: joyful time with the ones you love.

Chapter 9

Your Largest and Riskiest Investment

For the majority of practice owners, **the business** is not only their largest investment, but it is also the primary source for household income. In other words, it is an extremely valuable asset to the household. But until March of 2020, most practice owners didn't fully appreciate the risks of owning a small business. It took a government shutdown to show owners that owning a business can be extremely fragile if you are not able to treat patients. To be a Financial Beast, you must ensure you are building a business that is profitable, sustainable and valuable. It IS the engine to your household wealth and you must tap into its potential. Your attention should be focused on areas that will increase the value of the practice so when the day comes for you to transition out, you procure maximum value at sale. Let's call it what it is — you have put way too much time, attention, effort and investment into your practice only to let it sell for pennies on the dollar.

Just how risky is your healthcare practice? Let's look at some numbers. The S&P 500 Index represents 500 public companies. Many of you invest money in mutual funds that track this index. As of 4th QTR 2021, the S&P 500 had a Price to Earnings Ratio of 43. The price to earnings ratio measures the price of a company's shares relative to its earnings (profit). It is also referred to as an earnings multiple. The higher the multiple, the more confident investors are the company will produce profits and have a high rate of growth potential. It could also be an indicator that stocks are overvalued. Those of you who have bought or sold a practice, or have had a professional valuation, know the value of your business is largely based upon an earnings multiple. For most healthcare practice owners, that number is anywhere from 2 to 14 times. The difference is based upon a number of factors. Well-managed practices tend to be more profitable and will likely sell for a range of 8 to 12 times their earnings. Practices that are not well-managed will likely sell in the range of 2 to 6 times. If your business sold for a 5 times multiple, it is still 8 times riskier than putting your money into an S&P 500 Index fund.

I know many practice owners didn't get into healthcare just to make money. The care of patients and being able to control the quality of delivered medicine was equally important. But when you decided to own your own business, you made a commitment to the household to create an investment that could provide significant value. Most of you are in industries where private equity money is flowing and consolidation is occurring at electric speed. Whether you sell to a big corporation or to an associate, you should have your practice in a condition where you are able to recognize maximum value.

Your transition plan should have started the moment you opened your practice. It's never too late to put attention on some key areas which drive the most value in the business. Understand I am not just talking about monetary value. I am talking about time value, relationship value and the value of feeling less stress. These are the 5 key areas a buyer will inspect to determine how much they pay for your practice:

1. Organized Personnel. Your staff can be your most valuable resource or your biggest burden. You would be best served to hire staff who can be trained, have the willingness to work and can duplicate policies and procedures and who can use good judgement in their daily actions. The value of creating a good culture cannot be minimized. I have seen a $14 million sale get cancelled at the last minute because of one toxic staff member.

Key Stat: *Employee Turnover. 70% of staff would be long-term (over 3 years). Nobody will pay top dollar* *for a business where the people seem expendable and a team spirit is not being encouraged.*

2. Stable Practice Systems. This includes an automated marketing system, quality control system, management system, finance system, etc. No buyer will pay top dollar for a business built on a "hey you, go do this" method of management. Checklists, policies, procedures and an effective training system will allow for successful business expansion and a maximum value transition to new ownership.

Key Stat: *Ability to walk away from the business for 30 days without a significant drop in production.*

3. Viable Income Growth. No buyer will be willing to overpay for a business that is dying. Your business revenue cannot stay stagnate. To become a Financial Beast, you should be hitting a growth rate of 25% over a 3-year rolling period. In addition, you should have multiple income sources within the business. You should demonstrate an emphasis on those that are profitable, easy to deliver, and in highest demand. This would give a potential buyer confidence to offer a higher amount.

Key Stat: *Constant growth in new patients.*

4. Valuable Property Assets. Your business is made up of many things. Equipment, software, facility, etc.

All of these should be in good working condition. Your intellectual property should be protected, your corporate records should be updated every year, all your permits and licenses should be active, leaseholds should be favorable, there should be no unsettled legal issues, and your taxes should be paid. In addition, if you own a practice that relies on insurance reimbursements, you may want to pay a third party to audit the insurance contracts to ensure best practices are being followed. Legal rudiments can make or break you in a snap.

Key Stat: *Independent audit which indicates no compliance, HR or financial irregularities.*

5. Financial Solvency and Readiness. A top dollar buyer must see there is free flowing cash in the practice. In addition, all your financial reports (P&Ls, Balance Sheets, etc.) should be readily accessible, accurate and up to date. You should have zero business debt, no long-term commitments, no unusual arrangements, and nothing on the finance lines that could cause financial unpredictability. You should have plenty of business reserves (2 months of expenses) and maintain a profit margin of 20-30% (industry dependent).

Key Stat: *Adjusted Net Income (includes add backs) would be over 20%.*

Other Key factors which drive value:

- Your individual practice production should not exceed 20-25% of the practice production.

- The building or area would allow for expansion and added capacity.

- The online and community presence would indicate the practice is looked upon favorably.

- The practice is located in a growing population with high visibility and above average income range.

Your healthcare practice needs constant care and attention to reap its full financial benefits. You will need to plan reinvestment back into the practice to improve functionality and efficiency. These dollars are not wasted. If done correctly, you will get back 10 times what you put into it. Make your practice the largest, riskiest and MOST VALUABLE asset your household owns.

Chapter 10

The Value of Your 3 Roles

Your practice is a valuable investment. The roles you choose to play in the business will determine its value and whether you are able to harness its profit potential.

In my 13+ years working with owners, there were two common characteristics of those owners who built valuable businesses which translated into a personal financial success:

- They completely understood what role they needed to play to expand the practice.

- They compensated themselves correctly for all 3 roles.

I am sure you can remember the exact day and exact reason you decided to own your clinic. It was the glorious moment when you realized you didn't want to work for someone else, you could practice medicine your way and the financial rewards would always be greater. What's not to like? You failed to realize there were two other roles that were actually more important than being a doctor.

The three roles in your business are the Practitioner, the Executive and the Owner. The good news is each role has a certain compensation. The bad news is you must be competent at all three (or hire good people) to be successful.

Practitioner Role. This is the more natural role you play. You are a skilled caregiver delivering the services you spent 7 years or more to learn. The first responsibility is to be a top-notch doctor and to make sure your associates are competent at delivering high quality services. You should expect your associates to practice medicine based upon the standard of care you set forth. All your best practices should be codified so you can bring on other associates without sacrificing the quality of care.

Compensation: Most practice owners pay themselves a W-2 salary for the Practitioner role to cover their lifestyle expenses.

Executive Role. An Executive typically has the responsibility to manage others, ensure staff perform to expectations, and oversee the delivery of the company's product or service. This is not always the favorite role an Owner likes to play. Why? Most practitioners had little to no training on how to perform the duties of this role. This created a deficiency which allowed for only so much growth to occur before it stalled. Executives do not sit around in an office doing nothing. They are armed with checklists and are constantly inspecting different areas of the business to make sure the team is working together and keeping the show on the road. Having a competent executive team is a key component to expansion. Unfortunately, you may have to go through 10 to 20 employees to find one good executive. Trust me when I say, it is worth the wait. Pay them well when you find them.

Compensation: Most practice owners will take a % of the company profits in the form of a distribution for the Executive role. This is generally used to pay for the owner's lifestyle expenses.

Owner Role. The owner is the visionary who made a decision and took action to bring the practice into existence. They dreamed of how the practice would one day look. They established the purpose, the mission, and fulfilled the legal and financial requirements to start or acquire the business. When you opened your doors, the other roles began to eat up all your time. This caused you to neglect the Owner role. While it is the most important role you play, most do not understand the responsibilities and duties.

As an owner, you should be focusing most of your time on expansion activities, company culture, and business and regulatory compliance. In addition, you should ensure the business is compensating your household for all the risk you took for its creation. Most of you are drastically undercompensating yourself for this role.

MISSING Compensation: 10% of the Gross Revenue should be automatically and systematically channeled to the household to build income sources outside of the business.

Pick 2

While it's vital to understand the responsibilities of each of these roles, trying to play all 3 will make your head spin. **So pick two**. You can either be an Owner-Practitioner or Owner-Executive. I have seen it work either way. Whichever role you give up, make sure you hire a competent replacement. Keep in mind, your time is valuable so be sure to choose the role which is best for the business and your family.

As an owner, your financial responsibility is to ensure the business is providing maximum value for the benefit of the family. It is unfortunate that in your entire academic career, you were never taught these principles. Good thing it is never too late to learn.

To download The Econologics® 3 Roles of the Private Practice Owner chart, or to schedule a free 30-minute consultation, use this link or scan the QR code below: www.FinancialBeastBook.com

Chapter 11

The Golden Rules of Income and Expenses

There are natural laws of money. If you know them well, you can use them to your advantage. If you don't, you open yourself up to punishment. Just step off a cliff without a rope and witness the law of gravity. Claiming you weren't aware of gravity won't make the impact any less painful. The two most important natural laws of money are called ***"The golden rules of income and expenses."*** As a business owner, you must understand how they work or you will, sooner or later, suffer from financial insolvency.

It took me seven years, thousands of conversations, hours of analysis, and a few client failures to understand why most practice owners struggle to make payroll, have very little in personal and business reserves, have loads of bad debt, don't compensate themselves adequately, and tend to roll in and out of a cash flow crunch. There had to be some common denominator which would explain this phenomenon.

Finally, I was meeting with a physical therapy owner and it came to me. He had a $3,000,000 revenue PT Practice, but his staff wages were eating up most of his income and the amount he paid himself from the practice (around $500,000) barely paid for his lifestyle, taxes, and debt servicing. So I asked him how much income he REALLY needed to live the life he wanted. He looked puzzled, like I just stumped him with a trigonometry question. He finally said, "For me to really live the life I want to live, I need to make $1,500,000." Then I asked him how much the practice would need to produce for him to bring home $1,500,000 in profit to the household. He said around $7 to 8 million. The lightbulb went off in his head. I could actually see him working out what the practice would need to produce for him to hit this number. He worked out how many therapists he needed, how many patient visits he needed and what services he needed to add to hit his goal. Three years later, he hit his goal and his growth has increased each year since. I realized then, he intelligently applied both golden rules of income and expenses to solve his financial dilemma.

Golden Rule #1: Any business, organization, nation or household will try to SPEND every dollar that it makes — and then some.

There are so many examples of how this rule is true. Look no further than your practice. How many financial demands does your business have daily? How many people are always asking for more equipment, lower prices, better technology, more pay and benefits? The list goes on. Even at home you experience constant financial demands from your kids and spouse, house, taxes, vacation, etc. It is no wonder why most people don't have much in savings and have loads of debt. Do you ever look at your income and say, "Where did it all go?" It just seems to vanish.

The crazy thing is the amount of money you make really has no bearing on this truth. I have seen businesses which gross $500,000 a year and $10,000,000 million a year; both spend every cent. You have seen athletes, entertainers and lottery winners who have millions only to be broke some years later.

Groupthink is a powerful mechanism. As individuals, we are generally logical, sane and analytical in our thought process. As a group, the same does not apply. Groups must consume everything. It's an irrational manner of thinking but the group does not care. It thinks by spending everything they will be able to survive better. Unless you can separate yourself from the group mentality of "spend everything," you will always suffer the consequences.

Golden Rule #2: Any business, organization, nation or household will MAKE the precise amount of money it thinks it needs to cover its most vital expenses.

How many times have you been faced with a monumental expense that you knew you had to pay or else? How many times have you had payroll due in five days and had no idea how you would cover it? If you knew you needed $10,000 to cover a lifesaving surgery for your child, you can best believe you would find a way to make the money. People have this wonderful ability to create something out of nothing and overcome insurmountable barriers when pushed to the brink.

There is truth that as your need for something rises, your efforts will increase in order to match that need. It is called **necessity**. You have probably heard the phrase "necessity is the mother of invention." You have probably never heard the phrase "necessity is the sole driver of income." Both are true.

Necessity is defined as something that is urgently needed or required. It comes from the Latin *necedere: to not withdraw or yield*. There is something primal and barbaric about necessity. Think about our ancestors who needed to kill to eat or they starved. I am not saying you must be a bloodthirsty barbarian when it comes to income, but you do have to create a necessity for income to appear.

If the entire staff really believed that the company had to make 200 thousand per month to survive, amazingly they would produce $200,000 per month. If a person really believed he couldn't get by on less than $50,000 a month, that person would eventually make $50,000 a month. If you need to come up with $100,000 to save your child's life, come hell or high water, you would come up with the money. Necessity is what creates income.

Your practice will try and spend everything it makes AND will make the exact amount of money it thinks it needs to cover its most vital expenses.

So if you're wondering why you never seem to have much profit left at the end of the month, or why your financial reserves are so low, or why you never have enough to pay your tax bill, or why you always need to borrow money to expand — these golden rules explain it.

Here is how you apply these rules to your life to get into Financial Beast Mode:

HAVE ONE PERSON in charge of the finances of the practice. This person must have a bulldog mentality on collecting money, charging for services, controlling the expenses and have the ability to say "NO." You can try and run your finances by committee, but look how that worked for Congress; thirty trillion in debt and counting.

EXPENSE YOUR PROFITS. If you ever want to have any kind of financial future in which your household is NOT solely dependent on the practice income to thrive, then you will want to apply this step expertly. In other words, find a way to treat your practice profit as a vital and necessary expense to the business.

Keep reading this book to learn more about how to apply these principles.

Chapter 12

How to Correctly Expense your Profits as an Owner

The concept of treating your profits like an expense is not new, but the implementation is a bit misunderstood. I am not suggesting treating your profits like an expense to protect them from taxes. I am simply stating they need to be viewed by the business as a bill that needs to be paid EVERY WEEK. And like any other vital expense, it should be set up on an automatic and systematic method to pay without fail. It should be viewed no differently than your rent, your mortgage or utility bill.

Of all the concepts in this book, I can think of nothing more impactful then getting this implemented in your life and business. It solves so many of your money problems. It makes you feel like the business is FINALLY compensating you for all the years of hard work, money, blood, sweat and tears you have put in to sustain it. I have been lucky to witness the impact of this simple action on my clients. The vast majority went from having little in business reserves and personal investments to having hundreds of thousands to millions of dollars in the span of only 1 to 5 years. Witnessing the satisfaction from owners when they realize the fruits of their labor is truly empowering.

The "Expense Your Profits" Method in Practice

I was always baffled when I would ask practice owners what their make/break number was for the business. I would get a range of answers. Upon inspection, I did find out that most business owners only include their most basic expenses when calculating this number. This included rent, debt payments, marketing, salaries and overhead expenses. It did NOT include their actual owner compensation, their personal taxes, business savings or any money for expansion. It was no wonder they constantly had cash flow problems; their practice was operating on the wrong make/break number! The solution was to include "additional expenses" that the business was now forced to cover. The difference being these "expenses" actually created buffers for both the owner's household and their practice. It put pressure on the business to make more money and be more efficient. It also added to the overall value of the business while benefitting the household.

There are multiple methods of how to treat your profits as an expense. I am by no means saying this is the only way. It is a workable method.

First, I would recommend you set up five additional "Expense Accounts." All of these accounts have a very specific purpose and are super necessary.

Account #1 Wealth Storage Account: 10%. There is not a more important account you can set up than a Wealth Storage Account (WSA). This account is set up to capture the first 10% of practice revenue. This is your Owner Compensation. This is your compensation for the risk you took to put the practice in existence. I found it very surprising how few practice owners were doing this. I found it even more surprising how reluctant owners were to take this money. It's almost as if they were ashamed to take it. Like they did something wrong. Let me disabuse you of this idea once and for all:

- Who is personally responsible for all the debt payments?

- Who is responsible if there is a regulatory issue?

- Who is responsible if there is a lawsuit?

- Whose reputation is on the line if there is a public relations attack on the business?

Don't look too far because the answer is YOU!

There is no greater action you can take as a practice owner than to systematically take 10% of the practice revenue each week and channel it to a personal Wealth Storage Account (WSA).

The money in the WSA is specifically designed to be deployed to investment vehicles that can provide income to the household independent of the practice. You are likely to have many questions on this account such as: How do I set it up? Is it just a bank account? Do I hold it in the business? Where does the money get invested? What about the taxes? How do I tell my bookkeeper to classify this? I will provide more details on this in an upcoming chapter.

Account #2 Tax Account: 5-7%. Most practices are set up as an S Corp or an LLC taxed as an S Corp. Either way, you are personally liable for the income tax owed on the net profit of the business. If that is the case, you need to make sure there is money being expensed into a tax account to make sure you are paying your estimates timely. Your accountant should be able to provide the actual tax numbers. If you run a profitable business, then allocating 5-7% of your revenue to pay your taxes would seem prudent. If you are an S Corp, it doesn't really matter if the account is held in the business or personally, but you should always check with your tax professional to be sure. Having a good tax planner would be necessary to ensure not all the money in the tax account goes to the IRS. There are structures and strategies which can be set up to help you retain more of this money.

Account #3 Business Protection and Liability Account: 5%. Did you feel unprepared to have your practice shut down for just a matter of weeks? How do you feel when you have those 3-payroll months? Do you want to depend on a government bail out again? The risks a business owner has to confront are too many to count. You MUST be prepared for anything. The price of expansion is resistance, criticism and attack. It seems to be part of human nature. Whether it's a disgruntled employee or a regulatory agency, you have to be prepared to defend yourself. Having a minimum of two to three months of business expenses is a must for any practice. If you don't have it, then 5% of your revenues should be channeled into this type of account.

Account #4 Business Expansion Account: 3%. Believe it or not, you don't have to use debt for everything you want to buy. While there are times you need to use debt, you will most likely need to prove to the bank you are creditworthy and have good cash positions. In addition, you can put a higher down payment to potentially lower the liability and get a better interest rate. If you don't own your own building and would like to, the bank is likely going to ask for 25% down. Having a business expansion account can help plant the seeds for you having multiple locations and really growing your empire. In addition, you can reinvest this back into the business to create a better environment for your staff. This will go a long way in retaining productive and loyal staff.

Account #5 Celebration Account: 1%. We all need to blow off some steam from time to time. Plus, we need to make sure we validate our successes and celebrate wins. Does this mean you buy a $700,000 lake house? No. It does mean you need to blow money on something that makes you really happy and satisfied. One percent may not seem like a lot, but it could be an extra $30,000 to 40,000 to those with larger practices. That would pay for some fun trips!

To have any chance of financial freedom, you have to expense 98% of the money that your business brings in. Twenty to thirty percent of that expense should flow into these five accounts to ensure you can create a bright future.

You may be saying to yourself, there is no way I can allocate this much of my business revenue to match these percentages. You are correct. You are underestimating how much your make/break number actually needs to be to cover them.

Putting in this system of expensing your profits is not an easy endeavor. It is advisable to start your practice journey by implementing this method. In reality, anyone can do it at any time. Here are some best practices to make sure you are successful.

Expect massive pushback. Anytime you do something which will expand your net worth, you will likely not get much support. Expect to get very little support from your managers, employees or anyone else. Your accountant and financial professionals may even try and convince you not to do this. As crazy as that sounds, I have seen it happen more often than I would care to recall. Some people are so set in their ways, even constructive ideas are looked at with disdain.

Implement this on a gradient. While your business will eventually make the money to cover these "expenses," don't expect it to happen overnight. You don't want to overwhelm the business with these expenses when it is not accustomed to them. Start these flows at smaller amounts and gradually increase them every month until you reach the optimum percentages. This could take up to one year.

PUSH production and growth. Being able to put these accounts in place and have money flow into them means you have to be more aggressive and unreasonable about production and efficiency. Increase the speed in everything you and your staff do.

Don't be surprised if you find a person or two who is working against you. A financial destroyer HATES expansion. If you have this kind of toxic person in your environment, do everything within the law to get rid of that person ASAP.

Expensing your profits to create personal financial wealth is the most virtuous action you can do for the benefit of your family. Do it now!

Chapter 13

Get Your Numbers Right

Calculating your Household Income Target (HIT), Desired Minimum Monthly Income (DMMI) and Household Wealth Gap (HWG) is important.

Money is not wealth. If it were, we could just grant everyone $5,000,000 and all our problems would be over. Money is the result of providing exchangeable value to someone. Real wealth is owning things which produce goods and services.

Unfortunately, less than half of one percent of all Americans could financially survive if the stock market crashed 80%, inflation rose to 10%, a loved one was hit with a major health issue or they were decimated by a creditor attack. If there was a fundamental flaw in the way most people approach their finances, I would say it would be the underestimation of how much in income, assets and resources they actually need to live the life they want to live.

Far too many of us operate with the old school advice of saving "just enough" to pay for a basic lifestyle in retirement. Following that advice will potentially punish you by forcing you to live on a fixed income lifestyle. Like an engineer building a bridge, you must create a **factor of safety** in everything you do. That factor of safety as applied to your finances is key to your survival and must be built in NOW. A financial emergency can be defined as a predictable event that you failed to plan for. Allow me to elaborate:

Your Household Income Target (HIT): You will always have a problem with money if you don't figure out a way to make it. Sounds simple, but it's true. The reason most of us don't have enough income is because we drastically underestimate how much we actually need to fund our *ideal* lifestyle. The amount of money you make every month needs to cover three basic categories: current lifestyle, future wealth and play money.

Current Lifestyle. This includes your mortgage payments, debt payments, taxes, food, entertainment, kids, school, etc.

Future Wealth. Yes. You will need to build passive income for the future. This means that you should factor how much money you must invest in other income producing investments for the future income you need. In addition, this goal should be attained in less than 10 years.

Play Money. It's okay to have play money. It's healthy to want money to spend on things we want without feeling bad about spending it. You may have heard the term discretionary income, but I like play money better. It must be planned for.

Ninety percent of practice owners are making enough money to pay for their current lifestyle but are drastically deficient in the other two categories. That's the bad news. The good news is you know you can do something about it. Your business will provide for you if it is harnessed correctly.

Remember, you are not a rank-and-file worker who is operating on a fixed income. Start by looking at the three categories and figure out your correct HIT. Don't be overwhelmed if the number is double what you are making now. I'm guessing the amount of income you are making is 40-50% less than what you actually need. Know your number and don't settle for less. If you expect to become a Financial Beast, you should not have a HIT number LESS than $25,000 a month ($300,000 a year). You can have a lower Household Income Target, but it's very difficult to invest a significant amount towards future wealth, live a comfortable lifestyle and have play money. Financial Beasts compress the time it takes to get financially independent.

Calculate your Household Wealth Gap. Traditional retirement planning is becoming archaic. It's a game of accumulating "just enough" in reserves to replace 70-80% of your current income. The caveat is you can only withdrawal 4-5% of those reserves after age 60 or face the potential of running out of money. Does that sound like a safe financial condition to you? Plus, this backwards calculation doesn't take into consideration any outside factors like the tax effects of your investments, the risk of investment loss or any systemic risk (risk to our financial system) which could force you to live on less. This calculation may work for the typical employee, but not for you. You own a healthcare practice, and you need a calculation designed for your variable and increasing income. Let's start over with the correct way to calculate your Desired Monthly Minimum Income (DMMI).

The first question for this formula is: How much INCOME do you need to live the life you WANT to live? Forget the inflation factor or whatever other complex formulas get thrown at you. How much money, in today's dollars, do you want to have coming in to live your "ideal" lifestyle? It doesn't matter if the number is $20k, $30k, $50k, or $100k a month. Your number should factor in that you have MORE than enough to pay for whatever lifestyle you choose. This is THE most important number in the equation. Once you know your number then we can determine the total asset base needed to achieve the DMMI target. We do this by taking your Desired Income number and dividing it by 5%. We then subtract the value of your current assets from the asset base needed. This is your Household Value Gap. To repeat, once you determine how much in total assets you need to generate your DMMI, you then subtract the value of your current assets to figure out how much in value you need to create through continued savings, investment, and increased practice value.

Example:

- Desired Monthly Minimum Income: **$300,000** per year ($25,000 monthly)

- Total Asset Based Needed: $300,000/.05(5%) = **$6,000,000**

- Value of all current Household Assets (includes business, real estate, and other investments): **$3,500,000**

- Household Value Gap: Total Asset Base Needed ($6,000,000) – Value of current Household assets ($3,500,000) = **$2,500,000**

Do NOT underestimate your HIT, HWG or DMMI numbers. Make sure to factor all the unknown expenses life throws at you and the insanity of an overleveraged financial system.

Having correct financial targets is a necessity for you to become a Financial Beast. It allows you to put forth the correct amount of effort and intelligence needed to navigate a financial system that doesn't allow for a margin of safety. Don't play their game.

Chapter 14

A Practice Owner's Household Wealth Building Strategy

Ask 1000 people and you will garner 1000 different opinions on how to invest and build wealth. The internet is chock full of gurus, influencers, consultants and coaches who constantly sell the "secrets of the rich and wealthy." If there was a secret (which there isn't), then why is it so many have achieved a high level of wealth in so many different ways?

Instead of adding to the confusion, let's establish some fundamental agreements when it comes to investing and passive income:

- Having a household that has multiple income sources that are not all derived from "earned income" is desirable.

- Creating multiple and reliable income sources that can pay for one's basic lifestyle does not need to take a lifetime to achieve.

- Excess speculation when investing occurs when one does not have the discipline to follow a plan and often results in heavy losses.

- The key to building multiple income sources is to first focus on ONE income producing activity and make it as profitable and sustainable as possible. This will be the catalyst to build other income sources.

- Investing in assets which have the ability to create cash flow is a risk management approach which generally leads to success.

One thing we can all agree on is the traditional wealth building model of accumulating enough in retirement accounts which can replace 70–80% of your current income does not necessarily create a secure financial condition. It only takes one event to put your retirement accounts in peril.

A Financial Beast is not reliant on one of anything. The strategy outlined is not new nor is it particularly complex. The objective is to build multiple and reliable income sources to maximize the financial condition of the household. *This was designed specifically for practice owners.* Other small businesses who are in control of their company cash flow could copy this process. Hundreds of healthcare business owners are currently following this strategy and are achieving results. The effectiveness and workability are what determines the worthiness of this strategy.

I am in no way making any specific investment recommendations. The types of investments suggested here should be designed and applied prudently by professional and licensed advisors. Having an Econologics Financial Advisor assist you would increase the probability this gets implemented correctly.

The Parent Company: The Household

All your investments should provide some kind of a profit or value for the family unit. The goal should be to have enough reliable income sources where the household could financially survive in the event of an economic or social crisis.

Income Stream #1: The Practice. The business (or practices) is the main wealth building vehicle. Proper utilized, it provides profits to the parent company (household) which in turn allows the parent company to operate and expand. While the owner works in the practice as an Owner/Practitioner or Owner/Executive they are generally paid a W-2 salary which pays for the owner's lifestyle, taxes, and debt servicing. This salary ranges from $60,000 to $200,000. Profit distributions are also normally taken to handle any discretionary spending. A full 10% of the practice weekly revenues (not profit) are systematically withdrawn and allocated to the Wealth Storage Account. This is designated for investments to produce future income. Lastly, whenever the transition of the business takes place, the value of the practice sale would reflect it was treated as an investment and not a job.

Income Stream #2: The Practice Building. If possible, it is highly advisable to secure ownership of the real estate where your practice operates. The building would generally be owned in a separate business entity to reduce liability. A lease agreement should be in place where the practice pays the owners of the building (the Household) a fair market value rent which has a 2-3% annual increase. This will allow the owner to sell the practice and keep the real estate and the income it provides the household. It can provide a powerful tax benefit through an accelerated depreciation schedule.

Income Stream #3: The Wealth Storage Account (WSA). The Wealth Storage account is the hub of where the 10% of practice revenues will be channeled. As stated before, it is advisable to not start with a full 10% as the practice is not accustomed to this expense. A gradual payment should be started and increased every 4 to 5 weeks. This should be set up automatically and systematically. The Wealth Storage Account should be set up at a bank outside of your normal banking pattern. This discourages you from spending the money. As the money accumulates inside the WSA, it should be deployed into investment strategies that have the ability to provide cash flow. Enough cash should be held in the WSA to provide a 6-month to 1-year emergency fund for the household.

Income Stream #4: Public Securities. Stocks, Bonds, ETFs, Mutual Funds and other instruments which hold publicly traded securities can provide an income source for a household. These securities are usually held in a brokerage account with a reputable custodian. There are active and passive strategies which can be utilized. The allocation of assets is the most important factor when investing in these types of securities. An emphasis should be put on those instruments which provide dividends and yield potential. Far too many owners have misallocated their assets in the public security marketplace. This puts the household in jeopardy because of its risk factors and volatility. No more than 30% of the money being allocated in the WSA should be placed in public securities.

Income Stream #5: Insurance Products. This includes cash value life insurance and annuities. These products are offered through insurance companies. They are designed to provide guarantees, some tax advantages, liquidity and potentially income for life. Only highly rated insurance companies should be evaluated. There are many different kinds of insurance products so due diligence should be done before buying a product. The design, modification and funding of the policies are of the highest importance. Too many unscrupulous agents have sold unnecessary polices that were underutilized, which resulted in creating disrepute in an industry known for being an excellent steward of money. 30–40% of the WSA could be positioned in a proper strategy using these types of products.

Income Stream #6: Real Estate. Done correctly, investing in real estate can provide capital appreciation, income and excellent tax benefits. Done incorrectly, it can consume the attention of a household, force the owner to subsidize costs associated with the real estate, or overleverage and cause a bankruptcy situation. Research and due diligence should be done before buying any real estate. It will often be in the practice owner's best interest to either partner with someone who is a professional or find an operator who specializes in certain types of real estate and become a limited partner. Thirty to forty percent of the money in the Wealth Storage Account can be invested in the real estate markets. Just do so with great care.

Income Stream #7: Qualified Plans. Most owners have some type of Profit Sharing, 401k, SIMPLE IRA or Defined Benefit Plan set up through their office. Contributions are done through salary deferral and normally a company match is provided to all the participants. Far too many practice owners are dependent on their qualified plans for their retirement. In addition, most contributions are pre-tax which means the entire portfolio will be subject to the highest taxation (ordinary income) when distributions begin. Maximum funding a qualified plan is not harmful if other income streams are being built and a majority of the contributions are made post-tax if applicable.

Income Stream #8: Private Placements or Private Deals. Private placements are offerings of different kinds of private investments and unregistered securities to a limited pool of investors. One needs to be an accredited investor to participate in these types of offerings. The underlying strategies can include hedge funds, real estate, private lending, etc. Typically, your investments are illiquid. A high level of due diligence should be done on the sponsor or operator of the Private Placement Offering. Some offerings are high risk but also have the potential for high reward. You must trust the operator in these types of investments as they are responsible for all the decisions. Your involvement is that of a Limited Partner. This may shield you from any liability created by the sponsor. Your initial investment is the only asset at risk.

To recap the strategy:

- An automatic and systematic payment of 10% of the practice gross revenues should be paid weekly from the business checking account to an outside bank account designated as the Wealth Storage Account. Typically this is done as an ACH and is categorized as a profit distribution in QuickBooks or other bookkeeping program. This should be started on a gradient (small amount first and then gradually increasing) over the course of 6 to 10 months. The time frame is variable based upon circumstances.

- As money accumulates in the Wealth Storage Account, a deployment of that money should be structured to flow into public securities, insurance products and real estate. The amount for each strategy will vary due to circumstances but generally a 30/35/35 split has been workable. Please work with professional advisors before investing in each of those strategies.

- Every effort should be made to own the building where the practice resides. Make sure a lease agreement is in place between the practice and the entity which holds the real estate.

- If there is an existing Qualified Plan, every effort should be made to make it efficient, and the owner should begin contributing dollars in a post-tax manner (i.e. Roth 401k) to build tax advantaged income.

- The use of private placements should be used when the owner becomes an accredited investor but should be done in a prudent and responsible manner. The underlying investment strategy and the competency of the operator are the keys to success.

This is a much different approach than what you would hear from a typical wealth manager or CFP™ advisor. Becoming a Financial Beast means breaking from the norm so you can have an extraordinary financial experience.

To download the Econologics Wealth Building Blueprint, or to schedule a free 30-minute consultation, use this link or scan the QR code below: www.FinancialBeastBook.com

.

Chapter 15

The Difference Between Tactics and Strategy

Sun Tzu said, *"Strategy without tactics is the slowest route to victory. Tactics without strategy is the noise before defeat."* This quote really hit home when I first heard it. As I've mentioned before, I've had over 20,000 conversations with practice owners and almost all of them were operating on tactics without a strategy.

The most frustrating and time-consuming conversations I have with business owners is when the financial topic is centered around an activity that doesn't create a meaningful impact on the overall financial condition. This would include focusing on the last three-month performance of an individual investment or insurance product, obsessing over fees and credit scores, and discussions about a $5000 IRA contribution. In other words, I don't enjoy when the discussion is solely about *tactics*.

The most enlightening and enjoyable conversations I have with business owners is when the discussion is geared around big picture expansion, personal goals and methods of how to build wealth. In other words, I enjoy talking about **strategy**.

Strategy could be defined as a plan of action to achieve an overall goal or objective. Tactics are those actions which are taken which are designed to accomplish parts of the overall strategy. Don't get me wrong, taking it to the next level requires your understanding of strategy and tactics. The issue I have is when business owners spend FAR too much time on tactical actions they believe have more importance than the attainment of the overall strategy. What's worse is observing a business owner spending all their time chasing tactics with NO strategy.

Example: I recently spoke to a practice owner who could be best described as a "Know-it-All." You know the type. The guy or gal who thinks they know all there is to know. They believe you couldn't possibly tell them anything they "don't already know." He spent a good half-hour talking about his stock portfolio and how great of a business person he was, even though his profit was less than 10%. His questions were focused on fees, what products we sell and returns. This is the first sign of someone who has NO strategy and is utterly obsessed with tactics. The relevant questions should have been centered on our overall strategy to help him get to the next zone. Only after establishing the overall strategy would one focus on tactics.

It is difficult for me to blame the consumers for this obsession centered on tactics. Almost every blog, financial video, magazine or internet article on personal finances focuses primarily on the financial tactics one should implement. If you don't believe me, just go to YouTube and you will find the most popular videos consist of these topics: How to use a line of credit to pay off debt, how to buy real estate with no money down, how to pay off your student debt, what stocks to pick for growth, the best credit cards to apply for, banks that have the best yielding checking and savings accounts, how to travel the world for free, best investment for your Roth IRAs, the 10 best ways to save $1000 a year, and the list goes on and on.

These are all tactics. If you focus all your attention on tactics without following an overall strategy, you will lose the game of money. The financial elite are hoping for this. It should be no surprise why you are inundated with advertisements and information dealing mostly on financial tactics. They want you to buy their products.

Allow me to start the conversation off right and share with you the strategy of a Financial Beast.

Overall Objective: To run your personal finances like a business and to have a household that is in a financial condition at such a high level of abundance that it has income coming from multiple sources, no bad debt, there is a pool of money accumulated that can create a reliable income stream for life, all the household assets are reasonably protected from loss including taxes, inflation, and creditors, and death, the business is built for maximum value at sale, and the owner's time is free to pursue other life goals.

Overall Strategy: To produce enough income through multiple sources that will allow the household to live a comfortable lifestyle, build additional wealth with plenty of discretionary income, and the business is profitable, sustainable and transferable. To systematically channel a portion of the business profits to the household for the purpose of creating future income streams. To eradicate all bad debt and interest costs so the household is not overleveraged. To protect the assets of the household by ensuring that all the tax liabilities are kept to a minimum, a proper estate plan is in place, asset protection strategies are being implemented and there is a proper investment plan in place to ensure a legacy of wealth is being created and maintained.

Tactics
Work out how much income per month is needed for the household and then determine the precise amount of revenue the business needs to produce to maintain solvency.

Set up an outside bank account which will act as a Wealth Storage Account. Electronically link that account to the main business account and set up a systematic payment each week from the business account to the Wealth Storage account in the amount of 10% of the weekly business revenue.

Arrange a debt schedule to know with certainty when your bad debt will be eliminated and add an accelerator amount to pay the debt off sooner.

Reallocate certain investment accounts to reduce their overall risk of loss based upon a comparative analysis of the risk of the business and real estate holdings.

Get a Cost Segregation study done for the practice building to accelerate the tax benefits of the real estate.

Contact an attorney to update the business legal agreements and make sure all the basic estate planning documents are up to date and current.

This is the proper utilization of tactics in conjunction and in alignment with an overall strategy.

Most Investment advisors, tax advisors and insurance agents will do nothing but push tactics on you. I'm not saying tactics are bad, it's just the advice typically given is out of sequence and the important versus the unimportant activities are not clear because you are likely missing a strategy. You know it or you wouldn't be here reading this book on how to become a Financial Beast.

Chapter 16

How to Exit Your Business with Ease

Every healthcare practice owner will transition out of their business someday. That exit can be an exciting and profitable life event or end in regrettable shambles. It all depends on how much foresight is used to intelligently plan and execute the transition. You should have some idea how you will ultimately want to exit your business. Further, you will also want to be clear about what level of wealth you wish to acquire to pay for your standard of living throughout your life.

When a practice owner entertains the idea of exiting the practice, he has to look at the transaction from the perspective of the investor/owner or a fortune will be lost. Unfortunately, this is not a common practice since healthcare business owners are practitioners, not professional investors. There are successful actions that must be known and done to get the maximum value out of your investment. Otherwise, hundreds of thousands to millions of dollars can go unrealized.

Exit Options

Planning for your exit should start 10 years before you want to pull the trigger. That's right. And if you're within 10 years of retirement, start *right now!* Why? Because there are seven different strategies you can use to exit the practice and plenty of time would be needed to explore each option or combination of options to maximize the results of the exit. In his book, "Exiting Your Business, Protecting Your Wealth — A Strategic Guide for Owners and Their Advisors," John Leonetti lists the seven exit strategies, which are:

1. Die with Your Boots On

2. Close the Doors

3. Sell to a Competitor

4. Sell to a Corporate Group backed by Private Equity

5. Do an Associate/Manager Buy In or Buy Out

6. Employee Stock Ownership Plan

7. Gift to Charity or Children

Each of these strategies has pros and cons, especially in the valuation method used, terms of the sale and tax implications. The goal is to realize the maximum after-tax result that best furthers the goals of the exiting owner, while providing a winning solution for the buyer as well.

The financial condition of your household will have the biggest effect on what strategies you will be able to use; the less in financial resources you have outside the business, the less flexibility in the exit options available. If you have limited cash flow assets outside of your business, you may be relegated to choosing an option which may provide a win for you, but not the employees, the community or the patients.

Taxes

The sale of your practice will likely be the single largest financial transaction of your life. It may be an opportunity to cash in on a period of your life when you sacrificed to create something of value. That value, however, can be diminished by the income tax treatment of the sale to a greater or lesser degree by how the transaction is structured. This is another important reason why you should start your planning now. Tax laws change so you better be prepared to be ahead of the curve and have a plan you can pivot on when obstacles arise. When structuring a sale of a professional practice, it is advisable to include an accountant on your team to work out a more favorable tax treatment by analyzing the different taxable components of the enterprise prior to a transaction.

Because most practice owners will have very little cost basis (original value or purchase price of an asset), the majority of the sale proceeds will be taxed at capital gains rates. As of this time, the capital gains tax rate is 20%. In addition, you will need to pay the state tax which varies from state to state. This could be anywhere from 0–12% added on to the capital gains tax. There are legitimate solutions to minimizing the effect of the capital gains tax on your sale. If your accountant tells you to "just pay the tax" or "there are no strategies," it's time to get a second opinion. Usually, these options require you to give up some control of the proceeds either through the use of irrevocable trusts, charitable strategies or some type of installment sale. There is no free lunch. If you want to know how family offices ($100-million net worth or more) or billionaires structure their affairs, you have to be willing to play the same game.

Pulling the Trigger

There are two basic questions I would ask myself before I decide to sell:

1. Am I financially prepared to sell?

2. Am I emotionally prepared to sell?

Most business owners fail to realize how much cash flow and other benefits a business provides to their household. The cash flow created by the sales proceeds will likely never match the cash flow created while you own the business. ***One must do proper planning and income analysis*** to ensure the members of the household will be able to live their desired lifestyle based upon exiting the business. Working with an advisor who has navigated other clientele through similar situations is key. Your personal financial condition doesn't need to be perfect, but the sale proceeds should put you in a position where you have little to no destructive debt, multiple and reliable income sources, protected assets, and free range to pursue other endeavors.

Emotionally, the owner must have a new life planned out. You have spent almost 2/3 of your time and attention on this business for 10 to 20 years. Once you transition, an enormous amount of time will present itself for a short period. If you don't fill it with purposeful activities, it will get filled with something else. Nature abhors a vacuum. When someone doesn't have any real purpose, they start engaging in destructive activities. I have seen owners become grossly overweight, drink in excess and overspend their proceeds. All because they had no purposeful game to play.

NEVER MAKE A DECISION TO SELL IN BURNOUT!
If you've been in practice for any considerable amount of time, I'm sure you've had more than a few moments when you were just fed up. I mean COMPLETELY fed up! Staffing issues, long hours at the office, and attacks from disgruntled former employees finally convince you to throw in the towel. I get it.

This is your WARNING: do not make a huge financial decision like selling your business when you are in this emotionally bad place. NEVER make a financial decision when you are feeling overwhelmed or stressed. IF you do then the results could end up costing you MILLIONS. My advice? When faced with making a financial decision, look at the whole situation and how it would affect everyone in your life (including your employees and your patients). Make sure you have a good team of advisors who understand your specific business and are competent enough to help you navigate through this process. You want to choose people who have a track record of working with other business owners in your profession.

Getting the Highest Multiples

The number one question we get from a healthcare business owner thinking of selling in the near future is, "What factors bring the highest multiple?" Although not the only factors in the final sales price, in general the highest multiples will apply to the practice that can demonstrate these factors:

- At least 800+ EBITDA

- Employs over 4 producing practitioners

- Demographically favorable or in a high traffic area

- Exhibits a good online presence

- Practice is well known in the community

- Employs 1 to 3 tenured executives

- No major legal or compliance issues

- No one doctor is responsible for more than 25% of the total production

- The business has a consistent growth rate

- The facility has room for expansion.

The premium is paid to the least risky business venture. Multiples will generally start to come down as the buyer perceives you to have deficiencies in the above areas. This increases their risk and therefore the valuations will naturally come down. Not every practice will exhibit all these ideal factors, so don't be discouraged. Just be aware what will bring the highest multiple.

I find it amazing that practice owners will spend their entire career planning their business expansion and growth and wait until the very last minute to plan their exit. Starting now allows you time to distribute business profits to the household to create other income sources, eliminate your bad debt, and structure the practice so that it is worth the maximum value to another party.

This may seem a bit daunting to you, but it's easier than you think. To truly get into Financial Beast Mode the first step is to begin to think about the ideal exit and what kind of lifestyle you want to have after practice ownership. Get as specific as possible, then get to work taking on one detail at a time to create it. You'll be glad you did!

Chapter 17

Who Has Your Back?

I do understand the need to delineate out who is providing actual financial advice from those who are just pushing an insurance product, an investment product or any other "financial advice." I am just concerned that too many people are looking at an advisor who is a "fiduciary" and assuming that person is competent. It's too general of a term. Just because someone can pass a test or get a designation doesn't mean they are going to take you to the next level.

Does this mean I think you shouldn't work with a financial advisor who is acting under Fiduciary guidelines? No. It just shouldn't be the main criteria. If you are not paying a professional advisor for financial advice, you are likely not getting correct advice. Why? Because most professionals are motivated by how they are compensated. You should be willing to pay a competent advisor ANY price, if you feel he or she can help you achieve your optimum financial condition.

In the financial service industry, it seems that ROI (Return on Investment) or ROR (Rate of Return) is promoted literally. Whether it is a mutual fund portfolio, an annuity or a cash value life insurance policy, advisory clients look at their statements at the end of the year and evaluate the performance of that account relative to the advisor who set up the account. Most clients determine that the advisor is directly responsible for the success or failure of that investment and equate the advisor's worth on actual monetary returns. Here's a little-known fact: the financial advisor has very little to do with the performance of an account. Good performance of an investment account does not mean you have a competent advisor, and conversely just because an investment does not perform well, it does not necessarily mean your advisor is bad.

In my opinion, a great financial advisor should be a PRODUCT PUSHER. He should push his clients to follow a plan, get financial training and have more control. He should push his clients to produce more income, pay off their bad debt, minimize their taxes, increase their business value, protect their assets, create multiple income streams and invest correctly. A great financial advisor should use ALL TOOLS AND PRODUCTS AVAILABLE to help his clients reach the end goal.

The public at large doesn't trust financial advisors

because the majority of them don't get measurable and predictable results. This is the main problem. Most financial firms simply never defined the exact financial condition they are trying to help their clients obtain. They use words like "financial freedom" and "financial independence," but never give a precise definition what that means, nor the targets and financial metrics needed to measure this. Even fewer people have a trained advisor who holds you accountable for your actions.

So, what do you need to get help you get into Financial Beast mode?

You need a GUIDE. Not just any guide; you need a financial guide who understands the different levels of financial independence you can achieve, the different phases of your financial and business life, the potential obstacles and pitfalls you may encounter and how to navigate those obstacles so you can reach the next level.

Here are some of the criteria that I would look for when hiring a Financial Guide:

1. Do they communicate with the intent for me to understand? I am a simple guy. I don't enjoy when someone tries to talk over me or makes me feel like it's impossible to grasp something. I see this often in the financial industry. Accountants, economists, advisors, attorneys, and the like will sometimes try and use big words, nomenclature and other methods to confuse and control individuals. Any advisor you work with should have the basic intent of ensuring you completely understand whatever strategy or tactic they are recommending. If you walk out of a meeting with your advisor and feel like you have no idea what just happened or what your next action is, you may be working with the wrong person.

2. Do they have a basic financial philosophy which they base their strategies and systems on? Every science is built on basic fundamentals. The science of how to become financially independent is no different. Any guide you work with needs to have a basic philosophy that drives his or her recommendations. Here are some elements of our financial philosophy:

- Your household is the parent company and your personal finances should operate just like a business.

- Your attitude toward money will play a big part in your success with money.

- There are different levels of financial independence that have defined financial characteristics – know where you are and where you want to go.

- The individual can control his financial condition by engaging in constructive financial actions and repeat these actions over and over to get the best results.

- The formula for creating wealth is based upon the ability of the individual to acquire money, control money and expand money.

- The Optimum Financial Condition for a household is attainable and measurable and can be achieved by addressing the 9 key financial systems of the household.

- All assets, businesses and investments are owned or controlled by a household and should therefore serve and provide value for the goals and purposes of the household.

If you do not know the basic concepts and philosophies your financial advisor believes in, then he or she may guide you down a path you don't necessarily agree with.

3. Do they specialize in working with business owners and others in my professional industry? Once you truly grasp the concept that you should run your personal finances like a business, and the business is there to serve the household, you would NEVER choose a financial advisor who doesn't show you how to effectively utilize the business cash flow for the benefit of the Parent Company. Hundreds of thousands of dollars are lost because of this mistake. For most owners, the business and real estate make up about 90% of your overall net worth. I think it stands to reason that you should be working with a financial advisor who understands how 90% of your wealth impacts your life. Don't you?

4. Does the financial advisor have a financial planning system that keeps track of my key financial statistics and measures my results? You cannot manage something you cannot measure. This is where the consumers at large get duped. They think statistical measurements consist of the performance reports of their investment accounts. This is wholly incomplete. Any financial advisor you are working with should have at least 10 key financial metrics that not only report how your investments are doing, but also reflects how your financial BEHAVIOR is effecting your results. Any bull market and increase of one's assets due to market appreciation can mask massive financial irregularities and bad money behaviors. Objectively measurable and predictable financial metrics don't lie.

5. Does the advisor have expertise and a proven process that can help me no matter my financial condition or phase of ownership? Your financial life is not static. It is constantly in motion. If you think your financial life will be the same three months from now, you are sorely mistaken. Every household and every business owner goes through different phases which bring unique challenges. Your financial guide should have a system that helps you navigate through these different phases. So ask your advisor how they plan to help you ensure your wealth is managed properly — no matter where you are in your life and ownership cycle.

6. What kind of ongoing advisory system does my financial guide have to ensure I am progressing towards my financial goals? Meeting with an advisor once or twice a year to do a portfolio review is insufficient. Does your money take six months off? Ideally, the advisor would have a system consisting of having a monthly or quarterly meeting to evaluate the financial condition of the business and the household. You would be reviewing key financial statistics, (not just rates of return on investments), checklists of important financial actions and prioritizing activities that will result in efficient progress. Your financial advisor should be acting as your accountability coach.

So what kind of financial guide should you hire if you own a business? Here is my recommendation if you REALLY want to become a Financial Beast:

- The advisor should have a written statement that explains his or her basic philosophy on money and personal finances.

- The advisor should have a defined financial condition that he or she guides clients to progress toward.

- The advisor should be able to write a comprehensive financial plan that would outline an overall strategy and recommend the tactics used to achieve successful progression.

- The advisor should have list of financial metrics that are tracked and updated that objectively show client results.

- The advisor should have a follow-up system to ensure implementation and accountability.

- The advisor should offer, or have strategic partners who offer, suitable financial products and services that help the client tactically implement the overall strategy.

- The advisor should have experience working with the same or similar types of business owners in the client's professional industry.

- The advisor should have a written transition plan to assist the business owner in any phase of business ownership including a plan for the eventual exit out of the business.

- The advisor should have financial licensure and follow fiduciary standards to ensure he or she is following some regulatory compliance and best practices.

- The advisor should offer a robust financial education and training system to help the client make competent financial decisions.

Don't get too caught up in the "fiduciary" hype. It should never be the only criteria you look for when hiring a financial advisor. Go through these points and come up with your own criteria. Above all, you need to make sure your advisor is ethical, competent, and cares about seeing you win the financial game. Their actions will prove this point.

Chapter 18

The Measurements of a Financial Beast

In an effort to reduce the number of financial complexities you encounter on a daily basis, it is vital that you keep your attention focused on those actions that will provide the most favorable financial outcome. The only way to know if you are making real progress is to track effective measurements.

In the business world, these are known as Key Performance Indicators or KPIs. These are the indicators a business owner or manager should monitor to be able to evaluate the true direction and condition of an organization. Your household IS a business. There are household KPIs that every practice or business owner should track when it comes to their household finances. Remember, your business is generally the most valuable asset of the household and constant attention should be placed on increasing its value.

While I know all of you want to become Financial Beasts, my first target is to get you into Financial

Beast Mode. The difference will be apparent when reviewing the measurements below.

Household KPIs:

1. **Business Growth Rate (3 year rolling period)**

   The revenue growth of a business is a vital aspect of its overall value. You should always be pushing for an increase of expansion and business growth.

   Financial Beast Mode: 25% Business Growth Rate

   Financial Beast: 40% Business Growth Rate

2. **Weekly Business Revenue Reserved into Wealth Storage Account**

   This is the 10% of the business revenue that should be channeled into the household to create multiple income sources.

   Financial Beast Mode: 7–10% of weekly collections

   Financial Beast: Full 10%

3. **On Track to be Personally Debt Free**

   The goal is to eliminate all destructive, non-income producing debt as quickly as possible.

   Financial Beast Mode: 5–7 years

   Financial Beast: Personally debt free

4. Effective Tax Rate

This is percentage of the tax you pay compared to your personal gross income.

Financial Beast Mode: Under 30%

Financial Beast: Under 25%

5. Business Reserves

Every organization needs liquidity to handle business disruptions and attacks without being dependent on government programs.

Financial Beast Mode: 2 months of business expenses

Financial Beast: 3 months of business expenses

6. Asset Base for Passive Income

The goal for most practice owners is to have enough in assets that can generate enough reliable income to pay for their basic lifestyle. Using practice profits to build that asset base is ideal.

Financial Beast Mode: 30% of Asset base achieved

Financial Beast: 100% Asset base achieved

7. Business Profit Margin

The profit of the business will generally determine the multiple by which the practice is valued.

Financial Beast Mode: 20% Profit Margin

Financial Beast: 25% Profit Margin

8. Earned Income of the Household

To be able to live a comfortable lifestyle, invest for future income, and have play money, one needs to have an earned income target of over $300k.

Financial Beast Mode: Minimum of $300k

Financial Beast: Minimum of $400k

In addition, one should commit to some type of financial education or training every year. This could include weekend seminars, financial courses or timeless financial books.

There are other financial statistics to help you track your debt, insurance needs, asset protection and levels of investment risk. Having the correct financial metrics is vital to becoming a Financial Beast. This allows you to ignore distractions and focus on those activities that will let your financial score skyrocket.

To learn more about these and other financial statistics, or to schedule a free 30-minute consultation, use this link or scan the QR code below: www.FinancialBeastBook.com

Chapter 19

The Real Costs of Financial Freedom

I know I've covered a lot of information in this book but allow me to sum up the overall objective and strategy you should be striving for to become a Financial Beast.

Your Overall Goal: Attain at least Financial Zone 4 or higher.

Your Overall Strategic Objectives: To produce enough income that will allow your household to live a desired lifestyle, have discretionary income and a business that is profitable and sustainable. To have a system where a portion of the business profits are being channeled to the household, which will be utilized to create other income streams. To eradicate all bad debt and interest costs. To protect the assets of the household by ensuring tax liabilities are kept to a minimum, a proper estate plan is in place, assets are reasonably protected from lawsuits and over speculation, and time is created for the pursuit of enjoyment and other purposes.

So what are the actual costs to obtain financial freedom?

You may instantly think it would be hundreds of thousands of dollars over a 10 to 15 year period of investment and money management costs, insurance costs, legal and accounting costs, business consultants and other specialists. You would be wrong. The cost of financial freedom is not always a hard dollar cost. By definition, a cost does not necessarily need to be a monetary value. It is the effort, loss or sacrifice needed to obtain something.

The "costs" you can expect to spend on your journey are the time, effort and courage it takes to be financially aware and relentlessness.

#1: Constantly be Aware of Your Financial Condition.

Conditions in life change rapidly. It doesn't take long for any business or household that gets lazy or complacent on their finances to find themselves struggling, insolvent or falling short of their financial targets. Your financial awareness should be focused on 2 things:

1. The Optimum Financial Condition
2. Your Current Financial Condition

Only by knowing what your financial situation would ideally look like, can you then look at the state of your current finances and come up with a plan of attack. This is not an easy task. This is precisely why most people never make it. One simple action everyone can do is locate, identify and understand every asset and liability you currently have.

Financial awareness is keeping constant attention on the state of your finances and knowing what action steps need to be accomplished to bring more order and expansion. It creates necessity. Necessity is the voltage of financial growth.

#2: Be Relentless with Those Trying to Destroy Your Wealth.

You must be willing to stand up and fight against all the enemies of your financial success. There are the obvious enemies such as taxes, inflation, crony capitalism, government regulations and a flawed health insurance system. Many of you at times feel like you are helpless to fight against this economic system that is designed to keep you as a wage slave. You are NOT defenseless. You can control your sphere of influence. You can directly improve your financial situation by using some of tools in this book.

There are other financial destroyers. Unfortunately, they may be friends, family members, employees or advisors who "say" they are only looking out for you. Their real intentions are hidden. They do have characteristics:

- They tell you to stop working so hard and "enjoy life"

- They are routinely critical of you

- They constantly attract problems and conflict

- They are easily offended and always play the victim card

- They borrow and spend money without any care of consequences

- They often criticize or spread rumors about your most productive employees

- They are always blaming "the Economy" or someone else as the source of their failure

- They pressure you to invest in something they themselves have never invested in or done due diligence on

- They make you feel bad for being productive and having wealth

- They always talk about the "Pending Economic Collapse" and are obsessed with bad financial news

- They try to convince you to stay small and not expand

- They push prescription drugs and alcohol on you as a solution to your "financial stress"

Upon your inspection, you will find this person committing harmful if not criminal acts. They are writing bad checks, submitting false claims, channeling practice funds to themselves, giving away services, giving money to kids or lending money to others who cannot pay them back. Even if you have a great production month, they will always find fault with something you do.

There are probably many more indicators but the basic motives behind their actions are to:

- Make sure you are always in scarcity of money.

- Make sure you feel uncertain and unconfident about your ability to create financial independence.

Don't let these Financial Destroyers win. Be relentless with those who are trying to separate you from your wealth. Sometimes all it takes is simple communication to handle an attacker. Saying or doing something in opposition to those who are trying to destroy your wealth is the difference between you being a financial hero or a financial victim.

There are 7 billion people on the planet. Very few of us have the courage to take the level of action necessary to ensure we will be financially free.

I know you can be one of them. Pay the price now and live a life that you, your staff, your community and your family can be proud of.

Be Aware

Be Courageous

Be a Financial Beast!

ABOUT THE AUTHOR

Eric S. Miller

Financial Planning Expert for Healthcare Practice Owners

Specializing in the fields of Veterinary, Optometry, Physical Therapy, etc.

Eric Miller is a Registered Financial Consultant®, licensed insurance agent and a graduate of Capital University. He is a co-owner of Econologics Financial Advisors, LLC, a Registered Investment Advisory firm and national insurance agency where he serves as the Principal and Chief Financial Advisor. In 2019 and again in 2020, Econologics Financial Advisors was awarded the Inc. 5000 as one of the fastest growing companies in the US, which was a major accomplishment for Eric and the rest of the Econologics team.

As a 20+ year veteran of the financial planning profession, Eric has had the good fortune to work with over 500 healthcare business owners. In his tenure, he has dedicated his career to guiding his clients at every phase of ownership on how to be debt-free, invested, protected and set-for-life.

He and his team of advisors at Econologics Financial Advisor have been part of over 40 practice sales worth well over $230,000,000 collectively. Along with doing strategic financial planning, debt and credit management, asset protection, tax strategies and exit planning, they also manage or oversee close to $200,000,000 of client assets.

In addition to this book, Eric has published countless articles, videos and podcasts on various topics including how to avoid making the financial mistakes that trap owners. He has spoken at hundreds of live and virtual events nationwide as an expert on financial matters related to a practice owner's business and personal success.

Made in the USA
Monee, IL
12 November 2022